Ballast Water Management Convention
Convention sur la gestion des eaux de ballast
Convenio sobre la Gestión del Agua de Lastre

IMO INTERNATIONAL MARITIME ORGANIZATION

London, 2005

First published in 2005
by the INTERNATIONAL MARITIME ORGANIZATION
4 Albert Embankment, London SE1 7SR
www.imo.org

Printed in the United Kingdom by CPI Books Limited, Reading RG1 8EX

6   8   10   9   7

ISBN: 978-92-801-0033-4

IMO PUBLICATION
Sales number: I620M

This publication has been prepared from official documents of IMO, and every effort has been made to
eliminate errors and reproduce the original text(s) faithfully. Readers should be aware that, in case of
inconsistency, the official IMO text will prevail.

K48142

Foreword

The harmful effects of unwanted species in ships' Ballast Water was first reported to IMO in 1988, when Canada informed the Marine Environment Protection Committee (MEPC) about invasive aquatic species in the Great Lakes. In response, the MEPC adopted in 1991 the first voluntary guidelines for preventing the introduction into the marine environment of unwanted aquatic organisms and pathogens from ships' Ballast Waters and sediment discharges.

Following the UN Conference on Environment and Development (UNCED), held in Rio de Janeiro in 1992, the MEPC guidelines were reviewed and adopted as an Assembly resolution in 1993. The twentieth session of the IMO Assembly in 1997 adopted resolution A.868(20) "Guidelines for the control and management of ships' ballast water to minimize the transfer of harmful aquatic organisms and pathogens" which superseded earlier and less comprehensive guidelines. The new resolution requested Governments to take urgent action in applying the guidelines and to report any experience gained in their implementation to the MEPC. The resolution further requested the MEPC to work towards the completion of legally binding provisions on ballast water management together with guidelines for their uniform and effective implementation.

From 1999 onwards, the Ballast Water Working Group, established by MEPC in 1994, focused on the preparation of a free-standing Convention on control and management of ships' ballast water and sediments. In 2002, the World Summit on Sustainable Development held in Johannesburg, called for action at all levels to accelerate the development of measures to address invasive alien species in ballast water. The introduction of harmful aquatic organisms and pathogens to new environments has been identified as one of the four greatest threats to the world's oceans (the other three being land-sourced marine pollution, overexploitation of living marine resources and destruction of habitat). Proper control and management of ships' ballast water is therefore a major environmental challenge for IMO and the global shipping industry.

In accordance with Article 2(b) of the Convention on the International Maritime Organization, the Council agreed in principle to convene a diplomatic conference in 2003 to consider the adoption of the instrument. At its eighty-ninth session in November 2002, the Council reconsidered the matter, in view of the preparations made by MEPC, and approved the convening of the Diplomatic Conference in early 2004. The decision of the Council was endorsed by the twenty-third session of the Assembly in December 2003 and the International Conference on Ballast Water Management for Ships was held at IMO's Headquarters in London from 9 to 13 February 2004.

The Conference adopted the International Convention for the Control and Management of Ships' Ballast Water and Sediments (the Ballast Water Management Convention), together with four conference resolutions.

This publication contains the texts of the Convention and the four resolutions, aiming to provide an easy reference to administrators, shipowners, ship operators, port officers, seafarers and any other interested parties. It should be noted that, for legal purposes, the authentic text of the Convention should always be consulted.

Avant-propos

C'est en 1988 que les effets nuisibles des espèces indésirables dans les eaux de ballast des navires ont été signalés à l'OMI pour la première fois, lorsque le Canada a informé le Comité de la protection du milieu marin (MEPC) que des espèces aquatiques envahissantes se trouvaient dans les Grands Lacs. À la suite de cela, le MEPC a adopté en 1991 les premières directives facultatives visant à prévenir l'introduction dans le milieu marin d'organismes aquatiques et d'agents pathogènes indésirables par suite des rejets d'eaux de ballast et de sédiments par les navires.

À la suite de la Conférence des Nations Unies sur l'environnement et le développement (CNUED), tenue à Rio de Janeiro en 1992, les directives du MEPC ont été révisées et adoptées sous couvert d'une résolution de l'Assemblée en 1993. À sa vingtième session tenue en 1997, l'Assemblée de l'OMI a adopté la résolution A.868(20), intitulée «Directives relatives au contrôle et à la gestion des eaux de ballast des navires en vue de réduire au minimum le transfert d'organismes aquatiques nuisibles et d'agents pathogènes», laquelle a annulé et remplacé les précédentes directives qui étaient moins exhaustives. Cette nouvelle résolution priait les gouvernements de prendre de toute urgence des dispositions pour appliquer les directives et de rendre compte au MEPC de l'expérience acquise dans leur application. La résolution priait également le MEPC d'oeuvrer à la mise au point de dispositions juridiquement obligatoires sur la gestion des eaux de ballast et de directives pour leur application uniforme et effective.

À partir de 1999, les travaux du Groupe de travail sur les eaux de ballast, constitué par le MEPC en 1994, ont porté essentiellement sur l'élaboration d'une convention autonome pour le contrôle et la gestion des eaux de ballast et sédiments des navires. En 2002, le Sommet mondial pour le développement durable, tenu à Johannesburg, a demandé des actions à tous les niveaux pour accélérer la mise au point de mesures visant à trouver une solution au problème des espèces allogènes dans l'eau de ballast. L'introduction d'organismes aquatiques nuisibles et d'agents pathogènes dans de nouveaux environnements a été identifiée comme l'une des quatre plus grandes menaces posées aux océans du monde entier (les trois autres étant la pollution marine d'origine tellurique, la surexploitation des ressources marines biologiques et la destruction de l'habitat). La gestion et le contrôle adéquats des eaux de ballast des navires posent donc un important défi écologique à l'OMI et au secteur mondial des transports maritimes.

Conformément à l'article 2 b) de la Convention portant création de l'Organisation maritime internationale, le Conseil avait décidé en principe de convoquer en 2003 une conférence diplomatique chargée d'examiner l'adoption de l'instrument. À sa quatre-vingt-neuvième session tenue en novembre 2002, le Conseil a réexaminé la question, compte tenu des travaux préparatoires effectués par le MEPC, et a décidé que cette conférence diplomatique serait convoquée au début de 2004. L'Assemblée a entériné cette décision du Conseil à sa vingt-troisième session, en décembre 2003, et la Conférence internationale sur la gestion des eaux de ballast des navires s'est tenue au Siège de l'OMI, à Londres, du 9 au 13 février 2004.

La Conférence a adopté la Convention internationale pour le contrôle et la gestion des eaux de ballast et sédiments des navires (Convention sur la gestion des eaux de ballast), ainsi que quatre résolutions.

La présente publication contient le texte de la Convention et celui des quatre résolutions, dont l'objet est de fournir des références pratiques aux administrateurs, aux propriétaires et exploitants de navires, aux officiers de port, aux gens de mer et à toute autre partie intéressée. Il convient de noter que, à des fins juridiques, il faudrait toujours consulter le texte authentique de la Convention.

Prefacio

Los efectos perjudiciales de las especies no deseadas presentes en el agua de lastre de los buques se señalaron por primera vez a la OMI en 1988, cuando Canadá informó al Comité de Protección del Medio Marino (MEPC) de las especies acuáticas invasoras de los Grandes Lagos. La respuesta del MEPC fue adoptar en 1991 las primeras directrices voluntarias para impedir la introducción en el medio marino de organismos acuáticos no deseados y agentes patógenos procedentes de las descargas de agua de lastre y sedimentos de los buques.

Tras la Conferencia de las Naciones Unidas sobre el Medio Ambiente y el Desarrollo (CNUMAD), celebrada en Río de Janeiro en 1992, las directrices del MEPC se revisaron y se adoptaron como resolución de la Asamblea en 1993. En 1997, la Asamblea de la OMI, reunida en su vigésimo periodo de sesiones, adoptó la resolución A.868(20), titulada "Directrices para el control y la gestión del agua de lastre de los buques a fin de reducir al mínimo la transferencia de organismos acuáticos perjudiciales y agentes patógenos", que pasó a sustituir a las directrices anteriores, menos completas. En la nueva resolución se pedía a los Gobiernos que tomasen medidas urgentes para aplicar las directrices y que comunicasen al MEPC la experiencia que adquirieran mediante esa aplicación. En la resolución se pedía además al MEPC que trabajase con miras a ultimar disposiciones de obligado cumplimiento sobre la gestión del agua de lastre y directrices para la implantación efectiva y uniforme de dichas disposiciones.

A partir del año 1999, el Grupo de trabajo sobre el agua de lastre, que el MEPC había establecido en 1994, se centró en la elaboración de un convenio independiente sobre el control y la gestión del agua de lastre y los sedimentos de los buques. En 2002, la Cumbre Mundial sobre el Desarrollo Sostenible, celebrada en Johannesburgo, hizo un llamamiento para que se tomasen medidas a todos los niveles para acelerar la elaboración de soluciones al problema de las especies foráneas invasoras presentes en el agua de lastre. La introducción de organismos acuáticos perjudiciales y agentes patógenos en nuevos entornos constituye una de las cuatro grandes amenazas para los océanos del mundo (las otras son: la contaminación marina de fuentes terrestres, la sobreexplotación de los recursos vivos del mar y la destrucción de hábitats). Por ello, el adecuado control y gestión del agua de lastre de los buques representa un importante reto ambiental para la OMI y para el sector del transporte marítimo en todo el mundo.

De conformidad con lo dispuesto en el artículo 2 b) del Convenio constitutivo de la Organización Marítima Internacional, el Consejo decidió en principio celebrar una conferencia diplomática en 2003 para considerar la adopción del instrumento. En su 89º periodo de sesiones, celebrado en noviembre de 2002, el Consejo volvió a examinar esta cuestión en vista de los preparativos hechos por el MEPC y aprobó la celebración de la conferencia diplomática a principios de 2004. Esa decisión del Consejo fue refrendada por la Asamblea, reunida en vigésimo tercer periodo de sesiones, en diciembre de 2003, y la Conferencia internacional sobre la gestión del agua de lastre para buques se celebró en la sede de la OMI, en Londres, del 9 al 13 de febrero de 2004.

La Conferencia adoptó el Convenio internacional para el control y la gestión del agua de lastre y los sedimentos de los buques (Convenio sobre la Gestión del Agua de Lastre) y cuatro resoluciones.

La presente publicación contiene el texto del Convenio y las cuatro resoluciones a fin de facilitar un instrumento de fácil referencia para los administradores, los propietarios de buques, los armadores, los oficiales de puertos, la gente de mar y las demás partes interesadas. Cabe observar que, por motivos jurídicos, siempre debe consultarse el texto auténtico del Convenio.

Contents

International Convention for the Control and Management of Ships' Ballast Water and Sediments

Annex of Ballast Water Management Convention:
Regulations for the control and management of
ships' Ballast Water and Sediments

Appendices to annex

Resolutions

Table des matières

Annexe : *Règles pour le contrôle et la gestion*
des eaux de ballast et sédiments des navires

Appendices

Résolutions

Índice

INTERNATIONAL CONVENTION FOR THE CONTROL AND MANAGEMENT OF SHIPS' BALLAST WATER AND SEDIMENTS, 2004

THE PARTIES TO THIS CONVENTION,

RECALLING Article 196(1) of the 1982 United Nations Convention on the Law of the Sea (UNCLOS), which provides that "States shall take all measures necessary to prevent, reduce and control pollution of the marine environment resulting from the use of technologies under their jurisdiction or control, or the intentional or accidental introduction of species, alien or new, to a particular part of the marine environment, which may cause significant and harmful changes thereto",

NOTING the objectives of the 1992 Convention on Biological Diversity (CBD) and that the transfer and introduction of Harmful Aquatic Organisms and Pathogens via ships' ballast water threatens the conservation and sustainable use of biological diversity as well as decision IV/5 of the 1998 Conference of the Parties (COP 4) to the CBD concerning the conservation and sustainable use of marine and coastal ecosystems, as well as decision VI/23 of the 2002 Conference of the Parties (COP 6) to the CBD on alien species that threaten ecosystems, habitats or species, including guiding principles on invasive species,

NOTING FURTHER that the 1992 United Nations Conference on Environment and Development (UNCED) requested the International Maritime Organization (the Organization) to consider the adoption of appropriate rules on ballast water discharge,

MINDFUL of the precautionary approach set out in Principle 15 of the Rio Declaration on Environment and Development and referred to in resolution MEPC.67(37), adopted by the Organization's Marine Environment Protection Committee on 15 September 1995,

ALSO MINDFUL that the 2002 World Summit on Sustainable Development, in paragraph 34(b) of its Plan of Implementation, calls for action at all levels to accelerate the development of measures to address invasive alien species in ballast water,

CONSCIOUS that the uncontrolled discharge of Ballast Water and Sediments from ships has led to the transfer of Harmful Aquatic Organisms and Pathogens, causing injury or damage to the environment, human health, property and resources,

RECOGNIZING the importance placed on this issue by the Organization through Assembly resolutions A.774(18) in 1993 and A.868(20) in 1997, adopted for the purpose of addressing the transfer of Harmful Aquatic Organisms and Pathogens,

1

RECOGNIZING FURTHER that several States have taken individual action with a view to prevent, minimize and ultimately eliminate the risks of introduction of Harmful Aquatic Organisms and Pathogens through ships entering their ports, and also that this issue, being of worldwide concern, demands action based on globally applicable regulations together with guidelines for their effective implementation and uniform interpretation,

DESIRING to continue the development of safer and more effective Ballast Water Management options that will result in continued prevention, minimization and ultimate elimination of the transfer of Harmful Aquatic Organisms and Pathogens,

RESOLVED to prevent, minimize and ultimately eliminate the risks to the environment, human health, property and resources arising from the transfer of Harmful Aquatic Organisms and Pathogens through the control and management of ships' Ballast Water and Sediments, as well as to avoid unwanted side-effects from that control and to encourage developments in related knowledge and technology,

CONSIDERING that these objectives may best be achieved by the conclusion of an International Convention for the Control and Management of Ships' Ballast Water and Sediments,

HAVE AGREED as follows:

Article 1
Definitions

For the purpose of this Convention, unless expressly provided otherwise:

1   *Administration* means the Government of the State under whose authority the ship is operating. With respect to a ship entitled to fly a flag of any State, the Administration is the Government of that State. With respect to floating platforms engaged in exploration and exploitation of the sea-bed and subsoil thereof adjacent to the coast over which the coastal State exercises sovereign rights for the purposes of exploration and exploitation of its natural resources, including Floating Storage Units (FSUs) and Floating Production Storage and Offloading Units (FPSOs), the Administration is the Government of the coastal State concerned.

2   *Ballast Water* means water with its suspended matter taken on board a ship to control trim, list, draught, stability or stresses of the ship.

3   *Ballast Water Management* means mechanical, physical, chemical, and biological processes, either singularly or in combination, to remove, render harmless, or avoid the uptake or discharge of Harmful Aquatic Organisms and Pathogens within Ballast Water and Sediments.

4   *Certificate* means the International Ballast Water Management Certificate.

5   *Committee* means the Marine Environment Protection Committee of the Organization.

6   *Convention* means the International Convention for the Control and Management of Ships' Ballast Water and Sediments.

7   *Gross tonnage* means the gross tonnage calculated in accordance with the tonnage measurement regulations contained in Annex I to the International Convention on Tonnage Measurement of Ships, 1969 or any successor Convention.

8   *Harmful Aquatic Organisms and Pathogens* means aquatic organisms or pathogens which, if introduced into the sea, including estuaries, or into fresh water courses, may create hazards to the environment, human health, property or resources, impair biological diversity or interfere with other legitimate uses of such areas.

9   *Organization* means the International Maritime Organization.

10   *Secretary-General* means the Secretary-General of the Organization.

11   *Sediments* means matter settled out of Ballast Water within a ship.

12   *Ship* means a vessel of any type whatsoever operating in the aquatic environment and includes submersibles, floating craft, floating platforms, FSUs and FPSOs.

Article 2
General obligations

1   Parties undertake to give full and complete effect to the provisions of this Convention and the Annex thereto in order to prevent, minimize and ultimately eliminate the transfer of Harmful Aquatic Organisms and Pathogens through the control and management of ships' Ballast Water and Sediments.

2   The Annex forms an integral part of this Convention. Unless expressly provided otherwise, a reference to this Convention constitutes at the same time a reference to the Annex.

3   Nothing in this Convention shall be interpreted as preventing a Party from taking, individually or jointly with other Parties, more stringent measures with respect to the prevention, reduction or elimination of the transfer of Harmful Aquatic Organisms and Pathogens through the control and management of ships' Ballast Water and Sediments, consistent with international law.

4   Parties shall endeavour to co-operate for the purpose of effective implementation, compliance and enforcement of this Convention.

5   Parties undertake to encourage the continued development of Ballast Water Management and standards to prevent, minimize and ultimately eliminate the transfer of Harmful Aquatic Organisms and Pathogens through the control and management of ships' Ballast Water and Sediments.

6   Parties taking action pursuant to this Convention shall endeavour not to impair or damage their environment, human health, property or resources, or those of other States.

7   Parties should ensure that Ballast Water Management practices used to comply with this Convention do not cause greater harm than they prevent to their environment, human health, property or resources, or those of other States.

8   Parties shall encourage ships entitled to fly their flag, and to which this Convention applies, to avoid, as far as practicable, the uptake of Ballast Water with potentially Harmful Aquatic Organisms and Pathogens, as well as Sediments that may contain such organisms, including promoting the adequate implementation of recommendations developed by the Organization.

9   Parties shall endeavour to co-operate under the auspices of the Organization to address threats and risks to sensitive, vulnerable or threatened marine ecosystems and biodiversity in areas beyond the limits of national jurisdiction in relation to Ballast Water Management.

Article 3
Application

1   Except as expressly provided otherwise in this Convention, this Convention shall apply to:

(a)   ships entitled to fly the flag of a Party; and

(b)   ships not entitled to fly the flag of a Party but which operate under the authority of a Party.

2   This Convention shall not apply to:

(a)   ships not designed or constructed to carry Ballast Water;

(b)   ships of a Party which only operate in waters under the jurisdiction of that Party, unless the Party determines that the discharge of Ballast Water from such ships would impair or damage their environment, human health, property or resources, or those of adjacent or other States;

(c)   ships of a Party which only operate in waters under the jurisdiction of another Party, subject to the authorization of the latter Party for such exclusion. No Party shall grant such authorization if doing so would impair or damage their environment, human health, property or resources, or those of adjacent or other States. Any Party not granting such authorization shall notify the Administration of the ship concerned that this Convention applies to such ship;

(d)   ships which only operate in waters under the jurisdiction of one Party and on the high seas, except for ships not granted an authorization pursuant to subparagraph (c), unless such Party determines that the discharge of Ballast Water from such ships would impair or damage their environment, human health, property or resources, or those of adjacent of other States;

(e)   any warship, naval auxiliary or other ship owned or operated by a State and used, for the time being, only on government non-commercial service. However, each Party shall ensure, by the adoption of appropriate measures not impairing operations or operational capabilities of such ships owned or operated by it, that such ships act in a manner consistent, so far as is reasonable and practicable, with this Convention; and

(f) permanent Ballast Water in sealed tanks on ships, that is not subject to discharge.

3 With respect to ships of non-Parties to this Convention, Parties shall apply the requirements of this Convention as may be necessary to ensure that no more favourable treatment is given to such ships.

Article 4
Control of the transfer of Harmful Aquatic Organisms and Pathogens through ships' Ballast Water and Sediments

1 Each Party shall require that ships to which this Convention applies and which are entitled to fly its flag or operating under its authority comply with the requirements set forth in this Convention, including the applicable standards and requirements in the Annex, and shall take effective measures to ensure that those ships comply with those requirements.

2 Each Party shall, with due regard to its particular conditions and capabilities, develop national policies, strategies or programmes for Ballast Water Management in its ports and waters under its jurisdiction that accord with, and promote the attainment of the objectives of this Convention.

Article 5
Sediment reception facilities

1 Each Party undertakes to ensure that, in ports and terminals designated by that Party where cleaning or repair of ballast tanks occurs, adequate facilities are provided for the reception of Sediments, taking into account the guidelines developed by the Organization. Such reception facilities shall operate without causing undue delay to ships and shall provide for the safe disposal of such Sediments that does not impair or damage their environment, human health, property or resources or those of other States.

2 Each Party shall notify the Organization for transmission to the other Parties concerned of all cases where the facilities provided under paragraph 1 are alleged to be inadequate.

Article 6
Scientific and technical research and monitoring

1 Parties shall endeavour, individually or jointly, to:

(a) promote and facilitate scientific and technical research on Ballast Water Management; and

(b) monitor the effects of Ballast Water Management in waters under their jurisdiction.

Such research and monitoring should include observation, measurement, sampling, evaluation and analysis of the effectiveness and adverse impacts of any technology or methodology as well as any adverse impacts caused by such organisms and pathogens that have been identified to have been transferred through ships' Ballast Water.

2 Each Party shall, to further the objectives of this Convention, promote the availability of relevant information to other Parties who request it on:

(a) scientific and technology programmes and technical measures undertaken with respect to Ballast Water Management; and

(b) the effectiveness of Ballast Water Management deduced from any monitoring and assessment programmes.

Article 7
Survey and certification

1 Each Party shall ensure that ships flying its flag or operating under its authority and subject to survey and certification are so surveyed and certified in accordance with the regulations in the Annex.

2 A Party implementing measures pursuant to article 2.3 and Section C of the Annex shall not require additional survey and certification of a ship of another Party, nor shall the Administration of the ship be obligated to survey and certify additional measures imposed by another Party. Verification of such additional measures shall be the responsibility of the Party implementing such measures and shall not cause undue delay to the ship.

Article 8
Violations

1 Any violation of the requirements of this Convention shall be prohibited and sanctions shall be established under the law of the Administration of the ship concerned, wherever the violation occurs. If the Administration is informed of such a violation, it shall investigate the matter and may request the reporting Party to furnish additional evidence of the alleged violation. If the Administration is satisfied that sufficient evidence is available to enable proceedings to be brought in respect of the alleged violation, it shall cause such proceedings to be taken as soon as possible, in accordance with its law. The Administration shall promptly inform the Party that reported the alleged violation, as well as the Organization, of any action taken. If the Administration has not taken any action within one year after receiving the information, it shall so inform the Party which reported the alleged violation.

2 Any violation of the requirements of this Convention within the jurisdiction of any Party shall be prohibited and sanctions shall be established under the law of that Party. Whenever such a violation occurs, that Party shall either:

(a) cause proceedings to be taken in accordance with its law; or

(b) furnish to the Administration of the ship such information and evidence as may be in its possession that a violation has occurred.

3 The sanctions provided for by the laws of a Party pursuant to this article shall be adequate in severity to discourage violations of this Convention wherever they occur.

Article 9
Inspection of ships

1 A ship to which this Convention applies may, in any port or offshore terminal of another Party, be subject to inspection by officers duly authorized by that Party for the purpose of determining whether the ship is in compliance with this Convention. Except as provided in paragraph 2 of this article, any such inspection is limited to:

(a) verifying that there is on board a valid Certificate, which, if valid, shall be accepted; and

(b) inspection of the Ballast Water record book, and/or

(c) a sampling of the ship's Ballast Water, carried out in accordance with the guidelines to be developed by the Organization. However, the time required to analyse the samples shall not be used as a basis for unduly delaying the operation, movement or departure of the ship.

2 Where a ship does not carry a valid Certificate or there are clear grounds for believing that:

(a) the condition of the ship or its equipment does not correspond substantially with the particulars of the Certificate; or

(b) the master or the crew are not familiar with essential shipboard procedures relating to Ballast Water Management, or have not implemented such procedures;

a detailed inspection may be carried out.

3 In the circumstances given in paragraph 2 of this article, the Party carrying out the inspection shall take such steps as will ensure that the ship shall not discharge Ballast Water until it can do so without presenting a threat of harm to the environment, human health, property or resources.

Article 10
Detection of violations and control of ships

1 Parties shall co-operate in the detection of violations and the enforcement of the provisions of this Convention.

2 If a ship is detected to have violated this Convention, the Party whose flag the ship is entitled to fly, and/or the Party in whose port or offshore terminal the ship is operating, may, in addition to any sanctions described in article 8 or any action described in article 9, take steps to warn, detain, or exclude the ship. The Party in whose port or offshore terminal the ship is operating, however, may grant such a ship permission to leave the port or offshore terminal for the purpose of discharging Ballast Water or proceeding to the nearest appropriate repair yard or reception facility available, provided doing so does not present a threat of harm to the environment, human health, property or resources.

3   If the sampling described in article 9.1(c) leads to a result, or supports information received from another port or offshore terminal, indicating that the ship poses a threat to the environment, human health, property or resources, the Party in whose waters the ship is operating shall prohibit such ship from discharging Ballast Water until the threat is removed.

4   A Party may also inspect a ship when it enters the ports or offshore terminals under its jurisdiction, if a request for an investigation is received from any Party, together with sufficient evidence that a ship is operating or has operated in violation of a provision in this Convention. The report of such investigation shall be sent to the Party requesting it and to the competent authority of the Administration of the ship concerned so that appropriate action may be taken.

Article 11
Notification of control actions

1   If an inspection conducted pursuant to article 9 or 10 indicates a violation of this Convention, the ship shall be notified. A report shall be forwarded to the Administration, including any evidence of the violation.

2   In the event that any action is taken pursuant to article 9.3, 10.2 or 10.3, the officer carrying out such action shall forthwith inform, in writing, the Administration of the ship concerned, or if this is not possible, the consul or diplomatic representative of the ship concerned, of all the circumstances in which the action was deemed necessary. In addition, the recognized organization responsible for the issue of Certificates shall be notified.

3   The port State authority concerned shall, in addition to parties mentioned in paragraph 2, notify the next port of call of all relevant information about the violation, if it is unable to take action as specified in article 9.3, 10.2 or 10.3 or if the ship has been allowed to proceed to the next port of call.

Article 12
Undue delay to ships

1   All possible efforts shall be made to avoid a ship being unduly detained or delayed under article 7.2, 8, 9 or 10.

2   When a ship is unduly detained or delayed under article 7.2, 8, 9 or 10, it shall be entitled to compensation for any loss or damage suffered.

Article 13
Technical assistance, co-operation and regional co-operation

1   Parties undertake, directly or through the Organization and other international bodies, as appropriate, in respect of the control and management of ships' Ballast Water and Sediments, to provide support for those Parties which request technical assistance:

  (a) to train personnel;

  (b) to ensure the availability of relevant technology, equipment and facilities;

  (c) to initiate joint research and development programmes; and

  (d) to undertake other action aimed at the effective implementation of this Convention and of guidance developed by the Organization related thereto.

2   Parties undertake to co-operate actively, subject to their national laws, regulations and policies, in the transfer of technology in respect of the control and management of ships' Ballast Water and Sediments.

3   In order to further the objectives of this Convention, Parties with common interests to protect the environment, human health, property and resources in a given geographical area, in particular, those Parties bordering enclosed and semi-enclosed seas, shall endeavour, taking into account characteristic regional features, to enhance regional co-operation, including through the conclusion of regional agreements consistent with this Convention. Parties shall seek to co-operate with the Parties to regional agreements to develop harmonized procedures.

Article 14
Communication of information

1   Each Party shall report to the Organization and, where appropriate, make available to other Parties the following information:

  (a) any requirements and procedures relating to Ballast Water Management, including its laws, regulations, and guidelines for implementation of this Convention;

  (b) the availability and location of any reception facilities for the environmentally safe disposal of Ballast Water and Sediments; and

  (c) any requirements for information from a ship which is unable to comply with the provisions of this Convention for reasons specified in regulations A-3 and B-4 of the Annex.

2   The Organization shall notify Parties of the receipt of any communications under the present article and circulate to all Parties any information communicated to it under subparagraphs 1(b) and (c) of this article.

Article 15
Dispute settlement

Parties shall settle any dispute between them concerning the interpretation or application of this Convention by negotiation, enquiry, mediation, conciliation, arbitration, judicial settlement, resort to regional agencies or arrangements or other peaceful means of their own choice.

Article 16
Relationship to international law and other agreements

Nothing in this Convention shall prejudice the rights and obligations of any State under customary international law as reflected in the United Nations Convention on the Law of the Sea.

Article 17
Signature, ratification, acceptance, approval and accession

1　　This Convention shall be open for signature by any State at the Headquarters of the Organization from 1 June 2004 to 31 May 2005 and shall thereafter remain open for accession by any State.

2　　States may become Parties to the Convention by:

(a) signature not subject to ratification, acceptance, or approval; or

(b) signature subject to ratification, acceptance, or approval, followed by ratification, acceptance or approval; or

(c) accession.

3　　Ratification, acceptance, approval or accession shall be effected by the deposit of an instrument to that effect with the Secretary-General.

4　　If a State comprises two or more territorial units in which different systems of law are applicable in relation to matters dealt with in this Convention, it may at the time of signature, ratification, acceptance, approval, or accession declare that this Convention shall extend to all its territorial units or only to one or more of them and may modify this declaration by submitting another declaration at any time.

5　　Any such declaration shall be notified to the Depositary in writing and shall state expressly the territorial unit or units to which this Convention applies.

Article 18
Entry into force

1　　This Convention shall enter into force twelve months after the date on which not less than thirty States, the combined merchant fleets of which constitute not less than thirty-five percent of the gross tonnage of the world's merchant shipping, have either signed it without reservation as to ratification, acceptance or approval, or have deposited the requisite instrument of ratification, acceptance, approval or accession in accordance with article 17.

2   For States which have deposited an instrument of ratification, acceptance, approval or accession in respect of this Convention after the requirements for entry into force thereof have been met, but prior to the date of entry into force, the ratification, acceptance, approval or accession shall take effect on the date of entry into force of this Convention or three months after the date of deposit of instrument, whichever is the later date.

3   Any instrument of ratification, acceptance, approval or accession deposited after the date on which this Convention enters into force shall take effect three months after the date of deposit.

4   After the date on which an amendment to this Convention is deemed to have been accepted under article 19, any instrument of ratification, acceptance, approval or accession deposited shall apply to this Convention as amended.

Article 19
Amendments

1   This Convention may be amended by either of the procedures specified in the following paragraphs.

2   Amendments after consideration within the Organization:

(a) Any Party may propose an amendment to this Convention. A proposed amendment shall be submitted to the Secretary-General, who shall then circulate it to the Parties and Members of the Organization at least six months prior to its consideration.

(b) An amendment proposed and circulated as above shall be referred to the Committee for consideration. Parties, whether or not Members of the Organization, shall be entitled to participate in the proceedings of the Committee for consideration and adoption of the amendment.

(c) Amendments shall be adopted by a two-thirds majority of the Parties present and voting in the Committee, on condition that at least one third of the Parties shall be present at the time of voting.

(d) Amendments adopted in accordance with subparagraph (c) shall be communicated by the Secretary-General to the Parties for acceptance.

(e) An amendment shall be deemed to have been accepted in the following circumstances:

(i) An amendment to an article of this Convention shall be deemed to have been accepted on the date on which two thirds of the Parties have notified the Secretary-General of their acceptance of it.

(ii) An amendment to the Annex shall be deemed to have been accepted at the end of twelve months after the date of adoption or such other date as determined by the Committee. However, if by that date more than one third of the Parties notify the Secretary-General that they object to the amendment, it shall be deemed not to have been accepted.

(f) An amendment shall enter into force under the following conditions:

(i) An amendment to an article of this Convention shall enter into force for those Parties that have declared that they have accepted it six months after the date on which it is deemed to have been accepted in accordance with subparagraph (e)(i).

(ii) An amendment to the Annex shall enter into force with respect to all Parties six months after the date on which it is deemed to have been accepted, except for any Party that has:

(1) notified its objection to the amendment in accordance with subparagraph (e)(ii) and that has not withdrawn such objection; or

(2) notified the Secretary-General, prior to the entry into force of such amendment, that the amendment shall enter into force for it only after a subsequent notification of its acceptance.

(g) (i) A Party that has notified an objection under subparagraph (f)(ii)(1) may subsequently notify the Secretary-General that it accepts the amendment. Such amendment shall enter into force for such Party six months after the date of its notification of acceptance, or the date on which the amendment enters into force, whichever is the later date.

(ii) If a Party that has made a notification referred to in subparagraph (f)(ii)(2) notifies the Secretary-General of its acceptance with respect to an amendment, such amendment shall enter into force for such Party six months after the date of its notification of acceptance, or the date on which the amendment enters into force, whichever is the later date.

3   Amendment by a Conference:

(a) Upon the request of a Party concurred in by at least one third of the Parties, the Organization shall convene a Conference of Parties to consider amendments to this Convention.

(b) An amendment adopted by such a Conference by a two-thirds majority of the Parties present and voting shall be communicated by the Secretary-General to all Parties for acceptance.

(c) Unless the Conference decides otherwise, the amendment shall be deemed to have been accepted and shall enter into force in accordance with the procedures specified in paragraphs 2(e) and (f) respectively.

4   Any Party that has declined to accept an amendment to the Annex shall be treated as a non-Party only for the purpose of application of that amendment.

5   Any notification under this article shall be made in writing to the Secretary-General.

6   The Secretary-General shall inform the Parties and Members of the Organization of:

> **(a)** any amendment that enters into force and the date of its entry into force generally and for each Party; and
>
> **(b)** any notification made under this article.

Article 20
Denunciation

1   This Convention may be denounced by any Party at any time after the expiry of two years from the date on which this Convention enters into force for that Party.

2   Denunciation shall be effected by written notification to the Depositary, to take effect one year after receipt or such longer period as may be specified in that notification.

Article 21
Depositary

1   This Convention shall be deposited with the Secretary-General, who shall transmit certified copies of this Convention to all States which have signed this Convention or acceded thereto.

2   In addition to the functions specified elsewhere in this Convention, the Secretary-General shall:

> **(a)** inform all States that have signed this Convention, or acceded thereto, of:
>
> > **(i)** each new signature or deposit of an instrument of ratification, acceptance, approval or accession, together with the date thereof;
> >
> > **(ii)** the date of entry into force of this Convention; and
> >
> > **(iii)** the deposit of any instrument of denunciation from the Convention, together with the date on which it was received and the date on which the denunciation takes effect; and
>
> **(b)** as soon as this Convention enters into force, transmit the text thereof to the Secretariat of the United Nations for registration and publication in accordance with Article 102 of the Charter of the United Nations.

Article 22
Languages

This Convention is established in a single original in the Arabic, Chinese, English, French, Russian and Spanish languages, each text being equally authentic.

DONE AT LONDON this thirteenth day of February, two thousand and four.

IN WITNESS WHEREOF the undersigned* being duly authorized by their respective Governments for that purpose, have signed this Convention.

---

* Signatures omitted.

Annex
Regulations for the control and management of ships' Ballast Water and Sediments

SECTION A – GENERAL PROVISIONS

Regulation A-1
Definitions

For the purposes of this Annex:

1   *Anniversary date* means the day and the month of each year corresponding to the date of expiry of the Certificate.

2   *Ballast Water Capacity* means the total volumetric capacity of any tanks, spaces or compartments on a ship used for carrying, loading or discharging Ballast Water, including any multi-use tank, space or compartment designed to allow carriage of Ballast Water.

3   *Company* means the owner of the ship or any other organization or person such as the manager, or the bareboat charterer, who has assumed the responsibility for operation of the ship from the owner of the ship and who on assuming such responsibility has agreed to take over all the duties and responsibilities imposed by the International Safety Management Code.*

4   *Constructed* in respect of a ship means a stage of construction where:

  .1   the keel is laid; or

  .2   construction identifiable with the specific ship begins; or

  .3   assembly of the ship has commenced comprising at least 50 tonnes or 1 percent of the estimated mass of all structural material, whichever is less; or

  .4   the ship undergoes a major conversion.

5   *Major conversion* means a conversion of a ship:

  .1   which changes its ballast water carrying capacity by 15 percent or greater, or

  .2   which changes the ship type, or

  .3   which, in the opinion of the Administration, is projected to prolong its life by ten years or more, or

  .4   which results in modifications to its ballast water system other than component replacement-in-kind. Conversion of a ship to

---

* Refer to the ISM Code adopted by the Organization by resolution A.741(18), as amended.

15

meet the provisions of regulation D-1 shall not be deemed to constitute a major conversion for the purpose of this Annex.

6   *From the nearest land* means from the baseline from which the territorial sea of the territory in question is established in accordance with international law except that, for the purposes of the Convention, *from the nearest land* off the north-eastern coast of Australia shall mean from a line drawn from a point on the coast of Australia in

latitude 11°00′ S, longitude 142°08′ E
to a point in latitude 10°35′ S, longitude 141°55′ E
thence to a point latitude 10°00′ S, longitude 142°00′ E
thence to a point latitude 9°10′ S, longitude 143°52′ E
thence to a point latitude 9°00′ S, longitude 144°30′ E
thence to a point latitude 10°41′ S, longitude 145°00′ E
thence to a point latitude 13°00′ S, longitude 145°00′ E
thence to a point latitude 15°00′ S, longitude 146°00′ E
thence to a point latitude 17°30′ S, longitude 147°00′ E
thence to a point latitude 21°00′ S, longitude 152°55′ E
thence to a point latitude 24°30′ S, longitude 154°00′ E
thence to a point on the coast of Australia
in latitude 24°42′ S, longitude 153°15′ E.

7   *Active Substance* means a substance or organism, including a virus or a fungus, that has a general or specific action on or against Harmful Aquatic Organisms and Pathogens.

Regulation A-2
General applicability

Except where expressly provided otherwise, the discharge of Ballast Water shall only be conducted through Ballast Water Management in accordance with the provisions of this Annex.

Regulation A-3
Exceptions

The requirements of regulation B-3, or any measures adopted by a Party pursuant to article 2.3 and section C, shall not apply to:

   1   the uptake or discharge of Ballast Water and Sediments necessary for the purpose of ensuring the safety of a ship in emergency situations or saving life at sea; or

   2   the accidental discharge or ingress of Ballast Water and Sediments resulting from damage to a ship or its equipment:

      .1   provided that all reasonable precautions have been taken before and after the occurrence of the damage or discovery of the damage or discharge for the purpose of preventing or minimizing the discharge; and

      .2   unless the owner, Company or officer in charge wilfully or recklessly caused damage; or

3   the uptake and discharge of Ballast Water and Sediments when being used for the purpose of avoiding or minimizing pollution incidents from the ship; or

4   the uptake and subsequent discharge on the high seas of the same Ballast Water and Sediments; or

5   the discharge of Ballast Water and Sediments from a ship at the same location where the whole of that Ballast Water and those Sediments originated and provided that no mixing with un-managed Ballast Water and Sediments from other areas has occurred. If mixing has occurred, the Ballast Water taken from other areas is subject to Ballast Water Management in accordance with this Annex.

Regulation A-4
Exemptions

1   A Party or Parties, in waters under their jurisdiction, may grant exemptions to any requirements to apply regulations B-3 or C-1, in addition to those exemptions contained elsewhere in this Convention, but only when they are:

.**1**   granted to a ship or ships on a voyage or voyages between specified ports or locations; or to a ship which operates exclusively between specified ports or locations;

.**2**   effective for a period of no more than five years subject to intermediate review;

.**3**   granted to ships that do not mix Ballast Water or Sediments other than between the ports or locations specified in paragraph 1.1; and

.**4**   granted based on the guidelines on risk assessment developed by the Organization.

2   Exemptions granted pursuant to paragraph 1 shall not be effective until after communication to the Organization and circulation of relevant information to the Parties.

3   Any exemptions granted under this regulation shall not impair or damage the environment, human health, property or resources of adjacent or other States. Any State that the Party determines may be adversely affected shall be consulted, with a view to resolving any identified concerns.

4   Any exemptions granted under this regulation shall be recorded in the Ballast Water record book.

Regulation A-5
Equivalent compliance

Equivalent compliance with this Annex for pleasure craft used solely for recreation or competition or craft used primarily for search and rescue, less than 50 metres in length overall, and with a maximum Ballast Water Capacity of 8 cubic metres, shall be determined by the Administration, taking into account guidelines developed by the Organization.

SECTION B – MANAGEMENT AND CONTROL REQUIREMENTS FOR SHIPS

Regulation B-1
Ballast Water Management plan

Each ship shall have on board and implement a Ballast Water Management plan. Such a plan shall be approved by the Administration taking into account guidelines developed by the Organization. The Ballast Water Management plan shall be specific to each ship and shall at least:

> .1 detail safety procedures for the ship and the crew associated with Ballast Water Management as required by this Convention;
>
> .2 provide a detailed description of the actions to be taken to implement the Ballast Water Management requirements and supplemental Ballast Water Management practices as set forth in this Convention;
>
> .3 detail the procedures for the disposal of Sediments:
>
>> .1 at sea; and
>>
>> .2 to shore;
>
> .4 include the procedures for coordinating shipboard Ballast Water Management that involves discharge to the sea with the authorities of the State into whose waters such discharge will take place;
>
> .5 designate the officer on board in charge of ensuring that the plan is properly implemented;
>
> .6 contain the reporting requirements for ships provided for under this Convention; and
>
> .7 be written in the working language of the ship. If the language used is not English, French or Spanish, a translation into one of these languages shall be included.

Regulation B-2
Ballast Water record book

1   Each ship shall have on board a Ballast Water record book that may be an electronic record system, or that may be integrated into another record book or system and which shall at least contain the information specified in appendix II.

2   Ballast Water record book entries shall be maintained on board the ship for a minimum period of two years after the last entry has been made and thereafter in the Company's control for a minimum period of three years.

3   In the event of the discharge of Ballast Water pursuant to regulations A-3, A-4 or B-3.6 or in the event of other accidental or exceptional discharge of Ballast Water not otherwise exempted by this Convention, an entry shall be made in the Ballast Water record book describing the circumstances of, and the reason for, the discharge.

4   The Ballast Water record book shall be kept readily available for inspection at all reasonable times and, in the case of an unmanned ship under tow, may be kept on the towing ship.

5   Each operation concerning Ballast Water shall be fully recorded without delay in the Ballast Water record book. Each entry shall be signed by the officer in charge of the operation concerned and each completed page shall be signed by the master. The entries in the Ballast Water record book shall be in a working language of the ship. If that language is not English, French or Spanish the entries shall contain a translation into one of those languages. When entries in an official national language of the State whose flag the ship is entitled to fly are also used, these shall prevail in case of a dispute or discrepancy.

6   Officers duly authorized by a Party may inspect the Ballast Water record book on board any ship to which this regulation applies while the ship is in its port or offshore terminal, and may make a copy of any entry, and require the master to certify that the copy is a true copy. Any copy so certified shall be admissible in any judicial proceeding as evidence of the facts stated in the entry. The inspection of a Ballast Water record book and the taking of a certified copy shall be performed as expeditiously as possible without causing the ship to be unduly delayed.

Regulation B-3
Ballast Water Management for ships

1   A ship constructed before 2009:

> **.1**   with a Ballast Water Capacity of between 1,500 and 5,000 cubic metres, inclusive, shall conduct Ballast Water Management that at least meets the standard described in regulation D-1 or regulation D-2 until 2014, after which time it shall at least meet the standard described in regulation D-2;

> **.2**   with a Ballast Water Capacity of less than 1,500 or greater than 5,000 cubic metres shall conduct Ballast Water Management that at least meets the standard described in regulation D-1 or regulation D-2 until 2016, after which time it shall at least meet the standard described in regulation D-2.

2   A ship to which paragraph 1 applies shall comply with paragraph 1 not later than the first intermediate or renewal survey, whichever occurs first, after the anniversary date of delivery of the ship in the year of compliance with the standard applicable to the ship.

3   A ship constructed in or after 2009 with a Ballast Water Capacity of less than 5,000 cubic metres shall conduct Ballast Water Management that at least meets the standard described in regulation D-2.

4   A ship constructed in or after 2009, but before 2012, with a Ballast Water Capacity of 5,000 cubic metres or more shall conduct Ballast Water Management in accordance with paragraph 1.2.

5   A ship constructed in or after 2012 with a Ballast Water Capacity of 5,000 cubic metres or more shall conduct Ballast Water Management that at least meets the standard described in regulation D-2.

6   The requirements of this regulation do not apply to ships that discharge Ballast Water to a reception facility designed taking into account the guidelines developed by the Organization for such facilities.

7   Other methods of Ballast Water Management may also be accepted as alternatives to the requirements described in paragraphs 1 to 5, provided that such methods ensure at least the same level of protection to the environment, human health, property or resources, and are approved in principle by the Committee.

Regulation B-4
Ballast Water exchange

1   A ship conducting Ballast Water exchange to meet the standard in regulation D-1 shall:

   .1   whenever possible, conduct such Ballast Water exchange at least 200 nautical miles from the nearest land and in water at least 200 metres in depth, taking into account the guidelines developed by the Organization;

   .2   in cases where the ship is unable to conduct Ballast Water exchange in accordance with paragraph 1.1, such Ballast Water exchange shall be conducted taking into account the guidelines described in paragraph 1.1 and as far from the nearest land as possible, and in all cases at least 50 nautical miles from the nearest land and in water at least 200 metres in depth.

2   In sea areas where the distance from the nearest land or the depth does not meet the parameters described in paragraph 1.1 or 1.2, the port State may designate areas, in consultation with adjacent or other States, as appropriate, where a ship may conduct Ballast Water exchange, taking into account the guidelines described in paragraph 1.1.

3   A ship shall not be required to deviate from its intended voyage, or delay the voyage, in order to comply with any particular requirement of paragraph 1.

4   A ship conducting Ballast Water exchange shall not be required to comply with paragraphs 1 or 2, as appropriate, if the master reasonably decides that such exchange would threaten the safety or stability of the ship, its crew, or its passengers because of adverse weather, ship design or stress, equipment failure, or any other extraordinary condition.

5   When a ship is required to conduct Ballast Water exchange and does not do so in accordance with this regulation, the reasons shall be entered in the Ballast Water record book.

Regulation B-5
Sediment management for ships

1   All ships shall remove and dispose of Sediments from spaces designated to carry Ballast Water in accordance with the provisions of the ship's Ballast Water Management plan.

2   Ships described in regulation B-3.3 to B-3.5 should, without compromising safety or operational efficiency, be designed and constructed with a view to minimize the uptake and undesirable entrapment of Sediments, facilitate removal of Sediments, and provide safe access to allow for Sediment removal and sampling, taking into account guidelines developed by the Organization. Ships described in regulation B-3.1 should, to the extent practicable, comply with this paragraph.

Regulation B-6
Duties of officers and crew

Officers and crew shall be familiar with their duties in the implementation of Ballast Water Management particular to the ship on which they serve and shall, appropriate to their duties, be familiar with the ship's Ballast Water Management plan.

SECTION C – SPECIAL REQUIREMENTS IN CERTAIN AREAS

Regulation C-1
Additional measures

1   If a Party, individually or jointly with other Parties, determines that measures in addition to those in Section B are necessary to prevent, reduce, or eliminate the transfer of Harmful Aquatic Organisms and Pathogens through ships' Ballast Water and Sediments, such Party or Parties may, consistent with international law, require ships to meet a specified standard or requirement.

2   Prior to establishing standards or requirements under paragraph 1, a Party or Parties should consult with adjacent or other States that may be affected by such standards or requirements.

3   A Party or Parties intending to introduce additional measures in accordance with paragraph 1 shall:

    .1   take into account the guidelines developed by the Organization.

    .2   communicate their intention to establish additional measure(s) to the Organization at least 6 months, except in emergency or epidemic situations, prior to the projected date of implementation of the measure(s). Such communication shall include:

        .1   the precise co-ordinates where additional measure(s) is/are applicable;

.2 the need and reasoning for the application of the additional measure(s), including, whenever possible, benefits;

.3 a description of the additional measure(s); and

.4 any arrangements that may be provided to facilitate ships' compliance with the additional measure(s).

.3 to the extent required by customary international law as reflected in the United Nations Convention on the Law of the Sea, as appropriate, obtain the approval of the Organization.

4 A Party or Parties, in introducing such additional measures, shall endeavour to make available all appropriate services, which may include but are not limited to notification to mariners of areas, available and alternative routes or ports, as far as practicable, in order to ease the burden on the ship.

5 Any additional measures adopted by a Party or Parties shall not compromise the safety and security of the ship and in any circumstances not conflict with any other convention with which the ship must comply.

6 A Party or Parties introducing additional measures may waive these measures for a period of time or in specific circumstances as they deem fit.

Regulation C-2
Warnings concerning Ballast Water uptake in certain areas and related flag State measures

1 A Party shall endeavour to notify mariners of areas under their jurisdiction where ships should not uptake Ballast Water due to known conditions. The Party shall include in such notices the precise co-ordinates of the area or areas, and, where possible, the location of any alternative area or areas for the uptake of Ballast Water. Warnings may be issued for areas:

.1 known to contain outbreaks, infestations, or populations of Harmful Aquatic Organisms and Pathogens (e.g., toxic algal blooms) which are likely to be of relevance to Ballast Water uptake or discharge;

.2 near sewage outfalls; or

.3 where tidal flushing is poor or times during which a tidal stream is known to be more turbid.

2 In addition to notifying mariners of areas in accordance with the provisions of paragraph 1, a Party shall notify the Organization and any potentially affected coastal States of any areas identified in paragraph 1 and the time period such warning is likely to be in effect. The notice to the Organization and any potentially affected coastal States shall include the precise coordinates of the area or areas, and, where possible, the location of any alternative area or areas for the uptake of Ballast Water. The notice shall include advice to ships needing to uptake Ballast Water in the area, describing arrangements made for alternative supplies. The Party shall also notify mariners, the Organization, and any potentially affected coastal States when a given warning is no longer applicable.

Regulation C-3
Communication of information

The Organization shall make available, through any appropriate means, information communicated to it under regulations C-1 and C-2.

SECTION D – STANDARDS FOR BALLAST WATER MANAGEMENT

Regulation D-1
Ballast Water exchange standard

1   Ships performing Ballast Water exchange in accordance with this regulation shall do so with an efficiency of at least 95 percent volumetric exchange of Ballast Water.

2   For ships exchanging Ballast Water by the pumping-through method, pumping through three times the volume of each Ballast Water tank shall be considered to meet the standard described in paragraph 1. Pumping through less than three times the volume may be accepted provided the ship can demonstrate that at least 95 percent volumetric exchange is met.

Regulation D-2
Ballast Water performance standard

1   Ships conducting Ballast Water Management in accordance with this regulation shall discharge less than 10 viable organisms per cubic metre greater than or equal to 50 micrometres in minimum dimension and less than 10 viable organisms per millilitre less than 50 micrometres in minimum dimension and greater than or equal to 10 micrometres in minimum dimension; and discharge of the indicator microbes shall not exceed the specified concentrations described in paragraph 2.

2   Indicator microbes, as a human health standard, shall include:

   .1   Toxicogenic *Vibrio cholerae* (O1 and O139) with less than 1 colony-forming unit (cfu) per 100 millilitres or less than 1 cfu per 1 gram (wet weight) zooplankton samples;

   .2   *Escherichia coli* less than 250 cfu per 100 millilitres;

   .3   Intestinal Enterococci less than 100 cfu per 100 millilitres.

Regulation D-3
Approval requirements for Ballast Water Management systems

1   Except as specified in paragraph 2, Ballast Water Management systems used to comply with this Convention must be approved by the Administration taking into account guidelines developed by the Organization.

2   Ballast Water Management systems which make use of Active Substances or preparations containing one or more Active Substances to comply with this Convention shall be approved by the Organization, based on a procedure developed by the Organization. This procedure shall describe the approval and withdrawal of approval of Active Substances and their proposed manner of application. At withdrawal of approval, the use of the relevant Active Substance or Substances shall be prohibited within 1 year after the date of such withdrawal.

3   Ballast Water Management systems used to comply with this Convention must be safe in terms of the ship, its equipment and the crew.

Regulation D-4
Prototype Ballast Water treatment technologies

1   For any ship that, prior to the date that the standard in regulation D-2 would otherwise become effective for it, participates in a programme approved by the Administration to test and evaluate promising Ballast Water treatment technologies, the standard in regulation D-2 shall not apply to that ship until five years from the date on which the ship would otherwise be required to comply with such standard.

2   For any ship that, after the date on which the standard in regulation D-2 has become effective for it, participates in a programme approved by the Administration, taking into account guidelines developed by the Organization, to test and evaluate promising Ballast Water technologies with the potential to result in treatment technologies achieving a standard higher than that in regulation D-2, the standard in regulation D-2 shall cease to apply to that ship for five years from the date of installation of such technology.

3   In establishing and carrying out any programme to test and evaluate promising Ballast Water technologies, Parties shall:

    .1   take into account guidelines developed by the Organization, and

    .2   allow participation only by the minimum number of ships necessary to effectively test such technologies.

4   Throughout the test and evaluation period, the treatment system must be operated consistently and as designed.

Regulation D-5
Review of standards by the Organization

1   At a meeting of the Committee held no later than three years before the earliest effective date of the standard set forth in regulation D-2, the Committee shall undertake a review which includes a determination of whether appropriate technologies are available to achieve the standard, an assessment of the criteria in paragraph 2, and an assessment of the socio-economic effect(s) specifically in relation to the developmental needs of developing countries, particularly small island developing States. The Committee shall also undertake periodic reviews, as appropriate, to examine the applicable requirements for ships described in regulation B-3.1 as well as any other aspect of Ballast Water Management addressed in this Annex, including any guidelines developed by the Organization.

2   Such reviews of appropriate technologies shall also take into account:

.1   safety considerations relating to the ship and the crew;

.2   environmental acceptability, i.e., not causing more or greater environmental impacts than they solve;

.3   practicability, i.e., compatibility with ship design and operations;

.4   cost effectiveness, i.e., economics; and

.5   biological effectiveness in terms of removing, or otherwise rendering not viable, Harmful Aquatic Organisms and Pathogens in Ballast Water.

3   The Committee may form a group or groups to conduct the review(s) described in paragraph 1. The Committee shall determine the composition, terms of reference and specific issues to be addressed by any such group formed. Such groups may develop and recommend proposals for amendment of this Annex for consideration by the Parties. Only Parties may participate in the formulation of recommendations and amendment decisions taken by the Committee.

4   If, based on the reviews described in this regulation, the Parties decide to adopt amendments to this Annex, such amendments shall be adopted and enter into force in accordance with the procedures contained in article 19 of this Convention.

SECTION E – SURVEY AND CERTIFICATION REQUIREMENTS FOR BALLAST WATER MANAGEMENT

Regulation E-1
Surveys

1   Ships of 400 gross tonnage and above to which this Convention applies, excluding floating platforms, FSUs and FPSOs, shall be subject to surveys specified below:

.1   An initial survey before the ship is put in service or before the Certificate required under regulation E-2 or E-3 is issued for the first time. This survey shall verify that the Ballast Water Management plan required by regulation B-1 and any associated structure, equipment, systems, fitting, arrangements and material or processes comply fully with the requirements of this Convention.

.2   A renewal survey at intervals specified by the Administration, but not exceeding five years, except where regulation E-5.2, E-5.5, E-5.6, or E-5.7 is applicable. This survey shall verify that the Ballast Water Management plan required by regulation B-1 and any associated structure, equipment, systems, fitting, arrangements

25

and material or processes comply fully with the applicable requirements of this Convention.

.3 An intermediate survey within three months before or after the second anniversary date or within three months before or after the third anniversary date of the Certificate, which shall take the place of one of the annual surveys specified in paragraph 1.4. The intermediate surveys shall ensure that the equipment, associated systems and processes for Ballast Water Management fully comply with the applicable requirements of this Annex and are in good working order. Such intermediate surveys shall be endorsed on the certificate issued under regulation E-2 or E-3.

.4 An annual survey within three months before or after each anniversary date, including a general inspection of the structure, any equipment, systems, fittings, arrangements and material or processes associated with the Ballast Water Management plan required by regulation B-1 to ensure that they have been maintained in accordance with paragraph 9 and remain satisfactory for the service for which the ship is intended. Such annual surveys shall be endorsed on the Certificate issued under regulation E-2 or E-3.

.5 An additional survey, either general or partial, according to the circumstances, shall be made after a change, replacement, or significant repair of the structure, equipment, systems, fittings, arrangements and material necessary to achieve full compliance with this Convention. The survey shall be such as to ensure that any such change, replacement, or significant repair has been effectively made, so that the ship complies with the requirements of this Convention. Such surveys shall be endorsed on the Certificate issued under regulation E-2 or E-3.

2 The Administration shall establish appropriate measures for ships that are not subject to the provisions of paragraph 1 in order to ensure that the applicable provisions of this Convention are complied with.

3 Surveys of ships for the purpose of enforcement of the provisions of this Convention shall be carried out by officers of the Administration. The Administration may, however, entrust the surveys either to surveyors nominated for the purpose or to organizations recognized by it.

4 An Administration nominating surveyors or recognizing organizations to conduct surveys, as described in paragraph 3 shall, as a minimum, empower such nominated surveyors or recognized organizations[*] to:

.1 require a ship that they survey to comply with the provisions of this Convention; and

.2 carry out surveys and inspections if requested by the appropriate authorities of a port State that is a Party.

---

[*] Refer to the guidelines adopted by the Organization by resolution A.739(18), as may be amended by the Organization, and the specifications adopted by the Organization by resolution A.789(19), as may be amended by the Organization.

5   The Administration shall notify the Organization of the specific responsibilities and conditions of the authority delegated to the nominated surveyors or recognized organizations, for circulation to Parties for the information of their officers.

6   When the Administration, a nominated surveyor, or a recognized organization determines that the ship's Ballast Water Management does not conform to the particulars of the Certificate required under regulation E-2 or E-3 or is such that the ship is not fit to proceed to sea without presenting a threat of harm to the environment, human health, property or resources, such surveyor or organization shall immediately ensure that corrective action is taken to bring the ship into compliance. A surveyor or organization shall be notified immediately, and it shall ensure that the Certificate is not issued or is withdrawn as appropriate. If the ship is in the port of another Party, the appropriate authorities of the port State shall be notified immediately. When an officer of the Administration, a nominated surveyor, or a recognized organization has notified the appropriate authorities of the port State, the Government of the port State concerned shall give such officer, surveyor or organization any necessary assistance to carry out their obligations under this regulation, including any action described in article 9.

7   Whenever an accident occurs to a ship or a defect is discovered which substantially affects the ability of the ship to conduct Ballast Water Management in accordance with this Convention, the owner, operator or other person in charge of the ship shall report at the earliest opportunity to the Administration, the recognized organization or the nominated surveyor responsible for issuing the relevant Certificate, who shall cause investigations to be initiated to determine whether a survey as required by paragraph 1 is necessary. If the ship is in a port of another Party, the owner, operator or other person in charge shall also report immediately to the appropriate authorities of the port State and the nominated surveyor or recognized organization shall ascertain that such report has been made.

8   In every case, the Administration concerned shall fully guarantee the completeness and efficiency of the survey and shall undertake to ensure the necessary arrangements to satisfy this obligation.

9   The condition of the ship and its equipment, systems and processes shall be maintained to conform with the provisions of this Convention to ensure that the ship in all respects will remain fit to proceed to sea without presenting a threat of harm to the environment, human health, property or resources.

10   After any survey of the ship under paragraph 1 has been completed, no change shall be made in the structure, any equipment, fittings, arrangements or material associated with the Ballast Water Management plan required by regulation B-1 and covered by the survey without the sanction of the Administration, except the direct replacement of such equipment or fittings.

Regulation E-2
Issuance or endorsement of a Certificate

1   The Administration shall ensure that a ship to which regulation E-1 applies is issued a Certificate after successful completion of a survey conducted in accordance with regulation E-1. A Certificate issued under the authority of a Party shall be accepted by the other Parties and regarded for all purposes covered by this Convention as having the same validity as a Certificate issued by them.

2   Certificates shall be issued or endorsed either by the Administration or by any person or organization duly authorized by it. In every case, the Administration assumes full responsibility for the Certificate.

Regulation E-3
Issuance or endorsement of a Certificate
by another Party

1   At the request of the Administration, another Party may cause a ship to be surveyed and, if satisfied that the provisions of this Convention are complied with, shall issue or authorize the issuance of a Certificate to the ship, and where appropriate, endorse or authorize the endorsement of that Certificate on the ship, in accordance with this Annex.

2   A copy of the Certificate and a copy of the survey report shall be transmitted as soon as possible to the requesting Administration.

3   A Certificate so issued shall contain a statement to the effect that it has been issued at the request of the Administration and it shall have the same force and receive the same recognition as a Certificate issued by the Administration.

4   No Certificate shall be issued to a ship entitled to fly the flag of a State which is not a Party.

Regulation E-4
Form of the Certificate

The Certificate shall be drawn up in the official language of the issuing Party, in the form set forth in appendix I. If the language used is neither English, French nor Spanish, the text shall include a translation into one of these languages.

Regulation E-5
Duration and validity of the Certificate

1   A Certificate shall be issued for a period specified by the Administration that shall not exceed five years.

2   For renewal surveys:

   .1   Notwithstanding the requirements of paragraph 1, when the renewal survey is completed within three months before the expiry date of the existing Certificate, the new Certificate shall be valid from the date of completion of the renewal survey to a date not exceeding five years from the date of expiry of the existing Certificate.

.2   When the renewal survey is completed after the expiry date of the existing Certificate, the new Certificate shall be valid from the date of completion of the renewal survey to a date not exceeding five years from the date of expiry of the existing Certificate.

.3   When the renewal survey is completed more than three months before the expiry date of the existing Certificate, the new Certificate shall be valid from the date of completion of the renewal survey to a date not exceeding five years from the date of completion of the renewal survey.

3   If a Certificate is issued for a period of less than five years, the Administration may extend the validity of the Certificate beyond the expiry date to the maximum period specified in paragraph 1, provided that the surveys referred to in regulation E-1.1.3 applicable when a Certificate is issued for a period of five years are carried out as appropriate.

4   If a renewal survey has been completed and a new Certificate cannot be issued or placed on board the ship before the expiry date of the existing Certificate, the person or organization authorized by the Administration may endorse the existing Certificate and such a Certificate shall be accepted as valid for a further period which shall not exceed five months from the expiry date.

5   If a ship at the time when the Certificate expires is not in a port in which it is to be surveyed, the Administration may extend the period of validity of the Certificate, but this extension shall be granted only for the purpose of allowing the ship to complete its voyage to the port in which it is to be surveyed, and then only in cases where it appears proper and reasonable to do so. No Certificate shall be extended for a period longer than three months, and a ship to which such extension is granted shall not, on its arrival in the port in which it is to be surveyed, be entitled by virtue of such extension to leave that port without having a new Certificate. When the renewal survey is completed, the new Certificate shall be valid to a date not exceeding five years from the date of expiry of the existing Certificate before the extension was granted.

6   A Certificate issued to a ship engaged on short voyages which has not been extended under the foregoing provisions of this regulation may be extended by the Administration for a period of grace of up to one month from the date of expiry stated on it. When the renewal survey is completed, the new Certificate shall be valid to a date not exceeding five years from the date of expiry of the existing Certificate before the extension was granted.

7   In special circumstances, as determined by the Administration, a new Certificate need not be dated from the date of expiry of the existing Certificate as required by paragraph 2.2, 5 or 6 of this regulation. In these special circumstances, the new Certificate shall be valid to a date not exceeding five years from the date of completion of the renewal survey.

8   If an annual survey is completed before the period specified in regulation E-1, then:

> **.1**   the Anniversary date shown on the Certificate shall be amended by endorsement to a date which shall not be more than three months later than the date on which the survey was completed;

> **.2**   the subsequent annual or intermediate survey required by regulation E-1 shall be completed at the intervals prescribed by that regulation using the new Anniversary date;

> **.3**   the expiry date may remain unchanged provided one or more annual surveys, as appropriate, are carried out so that the maximum intervals between the surveys prescribed by regulation E-1 are not exceeded.

9   A Certificate issued under regulation E-2 or E-3 shall cease to be valid in any of the following cases:

> **.1**   if the structure, equipment, systems, fittings, arrangements and material necessary to comply fully with this Convention is changed, replaced or significantly repaired and the Certificate is not endorsed in accordance with this Annex;

> **.2**   upon transfer of the ship to the flag of another State. A new Certificate shall only be issued when the Party issuing the new Certificate is fully satisfied that the ship is in compliance with the requirements of regulation E-1. In the case of a transfer between Parties, if requested within three months after the transfer has taken place, the Party whose flag the ship was formerly entitled to fly shall, as soon as possible, transmit to the Administration copies of the Certificates carried by the ship before the transfer and, if available, copies of the relevant survey reports;

> **.3**   if the relevant surveys are not completed within the periods specified under regulation E-1.1; or

> **.4**   if the Certificate is not endorsed in accordance with regulation E-1.1.

Appendix I

Form of International Ballast Water Management Certificate

INTERNATIONAL BALLAST WATER MANAGEMENT CERTIFICATE

Issued under the provisions of the International Convention for the Control and Management of Ships' Ballast Water and Sediments (hereinafter referred to as "the Convention") under the authority of the Government of

. . . .

(full designation of the country)

by . . . .

(full designation of the competent person or organization authorized under the provisions of the Convention)

Particulars of ship*

Name of ship . . . .

Distinctive number or letters . . . .

Port of registry . . . .

Gross tonnage . . . .

IMO number[†] . . . .

Date of Construction . . . .

Ballast Water Capacity (in cubic metres) . . . .

Details of Ballast Water Management method(s) used

Method of Ballast Water Management used . . . .

Date installed (if applicable) . . . .

Name of manufacturer (if applicable) . . . .

---

[*] Alternatively, the particulars of the ship may be placed horizontally in boxes.
[†] IMO Ship Identification Number Scheme adopted by the Organization by resolution A.600(15).

The principal Ballast Water Management method(s) employed on this ship is/are:

☐ in accordance with regulation D-1

☐ in accordance with regulation D-2
(describe) . . . .

☐ the ship is subject to regulation D-4

THIS IS TO CERTIFY:

1   That the ship has been surveyed in accordance with regulation E-1 of the Annex to the Convention; and

2   That the survey shows that Ballast Water Management on the ship complies with the Annex to the Convention.

This Certificate is valid until . . . . subject to surveys in accordance with regulation E-1 of the Annex to the Convention.

Completion date of the survey on which this Certificate is based: dd/mm/yyyy

Issued at . . . .
(Place of issue of Certificate)

. . . .
(Date of issue)   *(Signature of authorized official issuing the Certificate)*

(Seal or stamp of the authority, as appropriate)

ENDORSEMENT FOR ANNUAL AND INTERMEDIATE SURVEY(S)

THIS IS TO CERTIFY that at a survey required by regulation E-1 of the Annex to the Convention the ship was found to comply with the relevant provisions of the Convention:

Annual survey: Signed . . . .
(Signature of duly authorized official)

Place . . . .

Date . . . .

(Seal or stamp of the authority, as appropriate)

Annual/Intermediate survey*:   Signed . . . .
(Signature of duly authorized official)

Place . . . .

Date . . . .

(Seal or stamp of the authority, as appropriate)

Annual/Intermediate survey*:   Signed . . . .
(Signature of duly authorized official)

Place . . . .

Date . . . .

(Seal or stamp of the authority, as appropriate)

Annual survey: Signed . . . .
(Signature of duly authorized official)

Place . . . .

Date . . . .

(Seal or stamp of the authority, as appropriate)

---

* Delete as appropriate.

33

ANNUAL/INTERMEDIATE SURVEY
IN ACCORDANCE WITH REGULATION E-5.8.3

THIS IS TO CERTIFY that, at an annual/intermediate* survey in accordance with regulation E-5.8.3 of the Annex to the Convention, the ship was found to comply with the relevant provisions of the Convention:

Signed . . . .
(Signature of duly authorized official)

Place . . . .

Date . . . .

(Seal or stamp of the authority, as appropriate)

ENDORSEMENT TO EXTEND THE CERTIFICATE IF VALID
FOR LESS THAN 5 YEARS WHERE REGULATION E-5.3 APPLIES

The ship complies with the relevant provisions of the Convention, and this Certificate shall, in accordance with regulation E-5.3 of the Annex to the Convention, be accepted as valid until . . . .

Signed . . . .
(Signature of duly authorized official)

Place . . . .

Date . . . .

(Seal or stamp of the authority, as appropriate)

ENDORSEMENT WHERE THE RENEWAL SURVEY HAS BEEN
COMPLETED AND REGULATION E-5.4 APPLIES

The ship complies with the relevant provisions of the Convention and this Certificate shall, in accordance with regulation E-5.4 of the Annex to the Convention, be accepted as valid until . . . .

Signed . . . .
(Signature of duly authorized official)

Place . . . .

Date . . . .

(Seal or stamp of the authority, as appropriate)

---

* Delete as appropriate.

ENDORSEMENT TO EXTEND THE VALIDITY OF THE CERTIFICATE UNTIL REACHING THE PORT OF SURVEY OR FOR A PERIOD OF GRACE WHERE REGULATION E-5.5 OR E-5.6 APPLIES

This Certificate shall, in accordance with regulation E-5.5 or E-5.6* of the Annex to the Convention, be accepted as valid until . . . .

Signed . . . .
(Signature of duly authorized official)

Place . . . .

Date . . . .

(Seal or stamp of the authority, as appropriate)

ENDORSEMENT FOR ADVANCEMENT OF ANNIVERSARY DATE WHERE REGULATION E-5.8 APPLIES

In accordance with regulation E-5.8 of the Annex to the Convention the new Anniversary date is . . . .

Signed . . . .
(Signature of duly authorized official)

Place . . . .

Date . . . .

(Seal or stamp of the authority, as appropriate)

In accordance with regulation E-5.8 of the Annex to the Convention the new Anniversary date is . . . .

Signed . . . .
(Signature of duly authorized official)

Place . . . .

Date . . . .

(Seal or stamp of the authority, as appropriate)

---

* Delete as appropriate.

35

Appendix II

Form of Ballast Water record book

INTERNATIONAL CONVENTION FOR THE CONTROL AND
MANAGEMENT OF SHIPS' BALLAST WATER AND SEDIMENTS

Period From: . . . . To: . . . .

Name of Ship . . . .

IMO number . . . .

Gross tonnage . . . .

Flag . . . .

Total Ballast Water Capacity (in cubic metres) . . . .

The ship is provided with a Ballast Water Management plan ☐

Diagram of ship indicating ballast tanks:

1   Introduction

In accordance with regulation B-2 of the Annex to the International Convention for the Control and Management of Ships' Ballast Water and Sediments, a record is to be kept of each Ballast Water operation. This includes discharges at sea and to reception facilities.

2   Ballast Water and Ballast Water Management

Ballast Water means water with its suspended matter taken on board a ship to control trim, list, draught, stability, or stresses of a ship. Management of Ballast Water shall be in accordance with an approved Ballast Water Management plan and taking into account guidelines[*] developed by the Organization.

---

[*] Refer to the Guidelines for the control and management of ships' ballast water to minimize the transfer of harmful aquatic organisms and pathogens adopted by the Organization by resolution A.868(20).

3   Entries in the Ballast Water record book

Entries in the Ballast Water record book shall be made on each of the following occasions:

3.1   When Ballast Water is taken on board:

.1   Date, time and location of port or facility of uptake (port or lat/long), depth if outside port

.2   Estimated volume of uptake in cubic metres

.3   Signature of the officer in charge of the operation.

3.2   Whenever Ballast Water is circulated or treated for Ballast Water Management purposes:

.1   Date and time of operation

.2   Estimated volume circulated or treated (in cubic metres)

.3   Whether conducted in accordance with the Ballast Water Management plan

.4   Signature of the officer in charge of the operation

3.3   When Ballast Water is discharged into the sea:

.1   Date, time and location of port or facility of discharge (port or lat/long)

.2   Estimated volume discharged in cubic metres plus remaining volume in cubic metres

.3   Whether approved Ballast Water Management plan had been implemented prior to discharge

.4   Signature of the officer in charge of the operation.

3.4   When Ballast Water is discharged to a reception facility:

.1   Date, time, and location of uptake

.2   Date, time, and location of discharge

.3   Port or facility

.4   Estimated volume discharged or taken up, in cubic metres

.5   Whether approved Ballast Water Management plan had been implemented prior to discharge

.6   Signature of officer in charge of the operation.

3.5   Accidental or other exceptional uptake or discharges of Ballast Water:

.1   Date and time of occurrence

.2   Port or position of the ship at time of occurrence

.3   Estimated volume of Ballast Water discharged

.4   Circumstances of uptake, discharge, escape or loss, the reason therefor and general remarks

.5   Whether approved Ballast Water Management plan had been implemented prior to discharge

.6   Signature of officer in charge of the operation.

3.6   Additional operational procedure and general remarks

4 Volume of Ballast Water

The volume of Ballast Water on board should be estimated in cubic metres. The Ballast Water record book contains many references to estimated volume of Ballast Water. It is recognized that the accuracy of estimating volumes of ballast is left to interpretation.

RECORD OF BALLAST WATER OPERATIONS

SAMPLE BALLAST WATER RECORD BOOK PAGE

Name of Ship: . . . .

Distinctive number or letters . . . .

Date	Item (number)	Record of operations/signature of officers in charge

Signature of master . . . .

ATTACHMENT

RESOLUTIONS ADOPTED BY THE CONFERENCE

Resolution 1

Future work by the Organization pertaining to the International Convention for the Control and Management of Ships' Ballast Water and Sediments

THE CONFERENCE,

HAVING ADOPTED the International Convention for the Control and Management of Ships' Ballast Water and Sediments (Convention),

NOTING that articles 5 and 9 and regulations A-4, A-5, B-1, B-3, B-4, B-5, C-1, D-3 and D-4 of the Annex to the Convention refer to guidelines or procedures to be developed by the Organization for the specific purposes identified therein,

RECOGNIZING the need for the development of these guidelines in order to ensure global and uniform application of the relevant requirements of the Convention,

INVITES the Organization to develop as a matter of urgency:

.1 Guidelines for sediment reception facilities under article 5 and regulation B-5;

.2 Guidelines for sampling of ballast water under article 9;

.3 Guidelines on ballast water management equivalent compliance for pleasure and search and rescue craft under regulation A-5;

.4 Ballast water management plan guidelines under regulation B-1;

.5 Guidelines for ballast water reception facilities under regulation B-3;

.6 Guidelines for ballast water exchange under regulation B-4;

.7 Guidelines for additional measures under regulation C-1 and for risk assessment under regulation A-4;

.8 Guidelines for approval of ballast water management systems under regulation D-3.1;

.9 Procedure for approval of active substances under regulation D-3.2; and

.10 Guidelines for prototype ballast water treatment technologies under regulation D-4,

and adopt them, as soon as practicable, and in any case before the entry into force of the Convention with a view to facilitating global and uniform implementation of the Convention.

Resolution 2

The use of decision-making tools when reviewing the standards pursuant to regulation D-5

THE CONFERENCE,

HAVING ADOPTED the International Convention for the Control and Management of Ships' Ballast Water and Sediments (Convention),

NOTING that regulation D-5 of the Convention requires that, at a meeting of the Marine Environment Protection Committee held no later than three years before the earliest effective date of the standard set forth in regulation D-2, the Committee shall undertake a review which includes a determination of whether appropriate technologies are available to achieve the standard, an assessment of the criteria in paragraph 2 of regulation D-5, and an assessment of the socio-economic effect(s) specifically in relation to the developmental needs of developing countries, particularly small island developing States,

RECOGNIZING the value of decision-making tools when preparing complex assessments,

RECOMMENDS the Organization to apply suitable decision-making tools when conducting the review of standards in accordance with regulation D-5 of the Convention; and

INVITES the Member States to advise the Organization on any relevant, robust decision-making tools to assist it in the conduct of such review.

Resolution 3

Promotion of technical co-operation and assistance

THE CONFERENCE,

HAVING ADOPTED the International Convention for the Control and Management of Ships' Ballast Water and Sediments (Convention),

BEING AWARE that Parties to the Convention will be called upon to give full and complete effect to its provisions, in order to prevent, minimize and ultimately eliminate the transfer of harmful aquatic organisms and pathogens through the control and management of ships' ballast water and sediments,

NOTING that the Convention provides in articles 13.1 and 13.2 for Parties, *inter alia*, to provide support for those Parties that request technical assistance in respect of the control and management of ships' ballast water and sediments,

RECOGNIZING the valuable technical co-operation activities undertaken in partnership with developing countries on Ballast Water Management issues under the GEF/UNDP/IMO Global Ballast Water Management Programme (GloBallast) since 2000,

BEING CONVINCED that the promotion of technical co-operation will expedite the acceptance, uniform interpretation and enforcement of the Convention by States,

NOTING WITH APPRECIATION that, through the adoption of resolution A.901(21), the Assembly of the International Maritime Organization (IMO):

(a) affirmed that IMO's work in developing global maritime standards and in providing technical co-operation for their effective implementation and enforcement can and does contribute to sustainable development; and

(b) decided that IMO's mission statement, in relation to technical co-operation in the 2000s, is to help developing countries improve their ability to comply with international rules and standards relating to maritime safety and the prevention and control of marine pollution, giving priority to technical assistance pro-grammes that focus on human resource development, particularly through training, and institutional capacity building;

1   REQUESTS Member States, in co-operation with IMO, other interested States and international bodies, competent international or regional organizations, and industry programmes, to promote and provide directly, or through IMO, support to States that request technical assistance for:

(a) the assessment of the implications of ratifying, accepting, approving, or acceding to, as well as implementing and enforcing the Convention;

(b) the development of national legislation and institutional arrangements to give effect to the Convention;

(c) the training of scientific and technical personnel for research, monitoring and enforcement (e.g., ballast water risk assessments, invasive marine species surveys, monitoring and early warning systems, ballast water sampling and analysis), including as appropriate the supply of necessary equipment and facilities, with a view to strengthening national capabilities;

(d) exchange of information and technical co-operation relating to minimization of risks to the environment and human health from transfer of harmful aquatic organisms and pathogens through the control and management of ships' ballast water and sediments;

(e) research and development of improved ballast water management and treatment methods; and

(f) establishment of special requirements in certain areas in accordance with Section C of the regulations of the Convention;

2   REQUESTS FURTHER international development agencies and organizations to support, including through the provision of necessary resources, technical co-operation programmes in the field of ballast water control and management, consistent with the Convention;

3   INVITES the Technical Co-operation Committee of IMO to continue providing for capacity-building activities on the control and management of ships' ballast water and sediments, within the Organization's Integrated Technical Co-operation Programme, in order to support the effective implementation and enforcement of the Convention by developing countries; and

4   URGES all States to initiate action in connection with the above-mentioned technical co-operation measures without awaiting the entry into force of the Convention.

Resolution 4

Review of the Annex to the International Convention for the Control and Management of Ships' Ballast Water and Sediments

THE CONFERENCE,

HAVING ADOPTED the International Convention for the Control and Management of Ships' Ballast Water and Sediments (Convention),

RECOGNIZING that review of the Annex to the Convention, and in particular but not restricted to regulations A-4, A-5, B-1, B-3, B-4, C-1, D-1, D-2, D-3 and D-5, may have to be considered prior to entry into force of the Convention, for instance, because of perceived impediments to entry into force or to address the standards set forth in regulation D-2 of the Annex to the Convention,

RECOMMENDS that the Marine Environment Protection Committee review the regulations of the Annex to the Convention as it considers appropriate, but not later than three years before the earliest effective date of the standards set forth in regulation D-2 of the Annex to the Convention, i.e., 2006.

CONVENTION INTERNATIONALE DE 2004 POUR LE CONTRÔLE ET LA GESTION DES EAUX DE BALLAST ET SÉDIMENTS DES NAVIRES

LES PARTIES À LA PRÉSENTE CONVENTION,

RAPPELANT l'article 196 1) de la Convention des Nations Unies de 1982 sur le droit de la mer, qui dispose notamment que «les États prennent toutes les mesures nécessaires pour prévenir, réduire et maîtriser la pollution du milieu marin résultant de l'utilisation de techniques dans le cadre de leur juridiction ou sous leur contrôle, ou l'introduction intentionnelle ou accidentelle en une partie du milieu marin d'espèces étrangères ou nouvelles pouvant y pro-voquer des changements considérables et nuisibles»,

NOTANT les objectifs de la Convention de 1992 sur la diversité biologique et le fait que le transfert et l'introduction d'organismes aquatiques nuisibles et d'agents pathogènes par les eaux de ballast des navires menacent la conser-vation et l'utilisation durable de la diversité biologique, ainsi que la déci-sion IV/5 concernant la conservation et l'utilisation durable des écosystèmes marins et côtiers, adoptée en 1998 par la Conférence des Parties à la Conven-tion sur la diversité biologique (COP 4), de même que la décision VI/23 concernant les espèces exotiques qui menacent des écosystèmes, des habi-tats ou des espèces, y compris les principes directeurs relatifs aux espèces envahissantes, adoptée en 2002 par la Conférence des Parties à la Conven-tion sur la diversité biologique (COP 6),

NOTANT AUSSI que la Conférence de 1992 des Nations Unies sur l'envi-ronnement et le développement (CNUED) avait prié l'Organisation maritime internationale («l'Organisation») d'envisager d'adopter des règles appropriées concernant le rejet des eaux de ballast,

AYANT À L'ESPRIT l'approche de précaution énoncée au Principe 15 de la Déclaration de Rio sur l'environnement et le développement et mentionnée dans la résolution MEPC.67(37), adoptée le 15 septembre 1995 par le Co-mité de la protection du milieu marin de l'Organisation,

AYANT À L'ESPRIT ÉGALEMENT que le Sommet mondial de 2002 pour le dé-veloppement durable a demandé, au paragraphe 34 b) de son Plan d'ap-plication, des actions à tous les niveaux pour accélérer la mise au point de mesures visant à trouver une solution au problème des espèces allogènes envahissantes rejetées dans l'eau de ballast,

CONSCIENTES que le rejet incontrôlé d'eaux de ballast et de sédiments par les navires a entraîné le transfert d'organismes aquatiques nuisibles et d'agents pathogènes qui portent atteinte ou nuisent à l'environnement, à la santé humaine, aux biens et aux ressources;

RECONNAISSANT l'importance que l'Organisation a donnée à cette question en adoptant les résolutions de l'Assemblée A.774(18) en 1993 et A.868(20)

en 1997 afin de traiter du transfert d'organismes aquatiques nuisibles et d'agents pathogènes,

RECONNAISSANT EN OUTRE que plusieurs États ont agi individuellement afin de prévenir, réduire au minimum et, en dernier ressort, éliminer les risques d'introduction d'organismes aquatiques nuisibles et d'agents pathogènes par les navires entrant dans leurs ports, et reconnaissant aussi que cette question, qui présente un intérêt mondial, nécessite la prise de mesures fondées sur des règles applicables à l'échelle mondiale et des directives pour l'application efficace et l'interprétation uniforme de ces règles,

DÉSIREUSES de voir se poursuivre la mise au point d'options de gestion des eaux de ballast plus sûres et plus efficaces qui permettront de prévenir, de réduire au minimum et, en dernier ressort, d'éliminer le transfert d'organismes aquatiques nuisibles et d'agents pathogènes,

RÉSOLUES à prévenir, réduire au minimum et, en dernier ressort, éliminer les risques pour l'environnement, la santé humaine, les biens et les ressources dus au transfert d'organismes aquatiques nuisibles et d'agents pathogènes, grâce au contrôle et à la gestion des eaux de ballast et sédiments des navires, tout en évitant les effets secondaires indésirables qu'un tel contrôle pourrait avoir, et à encourager l'évolution des connaissances et technologies connexes,

CONSIDÉRANT que le meilleur moyen d'atteindre ces objectifs est de conclure une Convention internationale pour le contrôle et la gestion des eaux de ballast et sédiments des navires,

SONT CONVENUES de ce qui suit :

Article 1
Définitions

Aux fins de la présente Convention, sauf disposition expresse contraire :

1　　*Administration* désigne le gouvernement de l'État sous l'autorité duquel le navire est exploité. Dans le cas d'un navire autorisé à battre le pavillon d'un État, l'Administration est le gouvernement de cet État. Dans le cas des plates-formes flottantes affectées à l'exploration et à l'exploitation des fonds marins et de leur sous-sol adjacents aux côtes sur lesquelles l'État côtier exerce des droits souverains aux fins de l'exploration et de l'exploitation de ses ressources naturelles, y compris les unités flottantes de stockage (FSU) et les unités flottantes de production, de stockage et de déchargement (FPSO), l'Administration est le gouvernement de l'État côtier intéressé.

2　　*Eaux de ballast* désigne les eaux et les matières en suspension prises à bord d'un navire pour contrôler l'assiette, la gîte, le tirant d'eau, la stabilité ou les contraintes.

3　　*Gestion des eaux de ballast* désigne les processus mécanique, physique, chimique et biologique utilisés, isolément ou parallèlement, pour éliminer ou rendre inoffensifs les organismes aquatiques nuisibles et les agents pathogènes présents dans les eaux de ballast et sédiments, ou à empêcher qu'ils soient admis dans ces eaux et sédiments ou rejetés avec ces eaux et sédiments.

4   *Certificat* désigne le Certificat international de gestion des eaux de ballast.

5   *Comité* désigne le Comité de la protection du milieu marin de l'Organisation.

6   *Convention* désigne la Convention internationale pour le contrôle et la gestion des eaux de ballast et sédiments des navires.

7   *Jauge brute* désigne la jauge brute calculée conformément aux règles sur le jaugeage des navires énoncées à l'Annexe I de la Convention internationale de 1969 sur le jaugeage des navires, ou dans toute convention qui lui succéderait.

8   *Organismes aquatiques nuisibles et agents pathogènes* désigne les organismes aquatiques et les agents pathogènes qui, s'ils sont introduits dans la mer, les estuaires ou les cours d'eau, peuvent mettre en danger l'environnement, la santé humaine, les biens ou les ressources, porter atteinte à la diversité biologique ou gêner toute autre utilisation légitime de ces milieux.

9   *Organisation* désigne l'Organisation maritime internationale.

10   *Secrétaire général* désigne le Secrétaire général de l'Organisation.

11   *Sédiments* désigne les matières provenant de l'eau de ballast qui se sont déposées à l'intérieur d'un navire.

12   *Navire* désigne un bâtiment de quelque type que ce soit exploité en milieu aquatique et englobe les engins submersibles, les engins flottants, les plates-formes flottantes, les FSU et les FPSO.

Article 2
Obligations générales

1   Les Parties s'engagent à donner pleinement effet aux dispositions de la présente Convention et de son Annexe afin de prévenir, de réduire au minimum et, en dernier ressort, d'éliminer le transfert d'organismes aquatiques nuisibles et d'agents pathogènes grâce au contrôle et à la gestion des eaux de ballast et sédiments des navires.

2   L'Annexe fait partie intégrante de la présente Convention. Sauf disposition expresse contraire, toute référence à la présente Convention constitue en même temps une référence à son Annexe.

3   Aucune disposition de la présente Convention ne doit être interprétée comme empêchant une Partie de prendre, individuellement ou conjointement avec d'autres Parties, des mesures plus rigoureuses destinées à prévenir, réduire ou éliminer le transfert d'organismes aquatiques nuisibles et d'agents pathogènes grâce au contrôle et à la gestion des eaux de ballast et sédiments des navires, en conformité avec le droit international.

4 Les Parties s'efforcent de coopérer afin de garantir la mise en oeuvre, l'observation et la mise en application effectives de la présente Convention.

5 Les Parties s'engagent à favoriser l'amélioration continue de la gestion des eaux de ballast et des normes visant à prévenir, réduire au minimum et, en dernier ressort, éliminer le transfert d'organismes aquatiques nuisibles et d'agents pathogènes grâce au contrôle et à la gestion des eaux de ballast et sédiments des navires.

6 Lorsqu'elles agissent en application de la présente Convention, les Parties s'efforcent de ne pas porter atteinte ni nuire à leur environnement, à la santé humaine, aux biens ou aux ressources, ou à ceux d'autres États.

7 Les Parties devraient veiller à ce que les pratiques de gestion des eaux de ballast utilisées pour satisfaire à la présente Convention n'entraînent pas plus de dommages qu'elles n'en préviennent pour leur environnement, la santé humaine, les biens ou les ressources, ou ceux d'autres États.

8 Les Parties encouragent les navires qui sont autorisés à battre leur pavillon et auxquels s'applique la présente Convention à éviter, dans la mesure où cela est possible dans la pratique, de prendre des eaux de ballast contenant des organismes aquatiques potentiellement nuisibles et des agents pathogènes, ainsi que des sédiments pouvant contenir de tels organismes, notamment en favorisant la mise en oeuvre satisfaisante des recommandations élaborées par l'Organisation.

9 Dans le contexte de la gestion des eaux de ballast, les Parties s'efforcent de coopérer, sous les auspices de l'Organisation, pour faire face aux menaces et aux risques qui pèsent sur les écosystèmes marins sensibles, vulnérables ou en danger et sur la diversité biologique, dans des zones situées au-delà des limites de la juridiction nationale.

Article 3
Champ d'application

1 Sauf disposition expresse contraire de la présente Convention, celle-ci s'applique :

a) aux navires qui sont autorisés à battre le pavillon d'une Partie; et

b) aux navires qui ne sont pas autorisés à battre le pavillon d'une Partie mais qui sont exploités sous l'autorité d'une Partie.

2 La présente Convention ne s'applique pas :

a) aux navires qui ne sont pas conçus ou construits pour transporter des eaux de ballast;

b) aux navires d'une Partie qui sont exploités uniquement dans les eaux relevant de la juridiction de cette Partie, à moins que celle-ci ne décide que le rejet d'eaux de ballast par de tels navires porterait atteinte ou nuirait à son environnement, à la santé humaine, aux biens ou aux ressources, ou à ceux d'États adjacents ou d'autres États;

c) aux navires d'une Partie qui sont exploités uniquement dans les eaux relevant de la juridiction d'une autre Partie, à condition que cette exclusion soit autorisée par la seconde Partie. Une Partie ne doit en aucun cas accorder une telle autorisation si cela risque de porter atteinte ou nuire à son environnement, à la santé humaine, aux biens ou aux ressources, ou à ceux d'États adjacents ou d'autres États. Toute Partie qui refuse d'accorder une telle autorisation doit notifier à l'Administration du navire intéressé que la présente Convention s'applique au navire en question;

d) aux navires qui sont exploités uniquement dans les eaux relevant de la juridiction d'une Partie et en haute mer, à l'exception de ceux auxquels une autorisation visée à l'alinéa c) ci-dessus n'a pas été accordée, à moins que cette Partie ne décide que le rejet d'eaux de ballast par de tels navires porterait atteinte ou nuirait à son environnement, à la santé humaine, aux biens ou aux ressources, ou à ceux d'États adjacents ou d'autres États;

e) aux navires de guerre, aux navires de guerre auxiliaires ou autres navires appartenant à un État ou exploités par lui et utilisés exclusivement, à l'époque considérée, pour un service public non commercial. Cependant, chaque Partie s'assure, en prenant des mesures appropriées qui ne compromettent pas les opérations ou la capacité opérationnelle des navires de ce type lui appartenant ou exploités par elle, que ceux-ci agissent d'une manière compatible avec la présente Convention, pour autant que cela soit raisonnable et possible dans la pratique ; et

f) aux eaux de ballast permanentes dans des citernes scellées à bord des navires, qui ne font pas l'objet d'un rejet.

3 Dans le cas des navires d'États non Parties à la présente Convention, les Parties appliquent les prescriptions de la présente Convention dans la mesure nécessaire pour que ces navires ne bénéficient pas d'un traitement plus favorable.

Article 4
Mesures de contrôle du transfert d'organismes aquatiques nuisibles et d'agents pathogènes par les eaux de ballast et sédiments des navires

1 Chaque Partie exige que les navires auxquels la présente Convention s'applique, et qui sont autorisés à battre son pavillon ou sont exploités sous son autorité, respectent les prescriptions de la présente Convention, y compris les normes et prescriptions applicables de l'Annexe, et prend des mesures effectives pour veiller à ce que ces navires satisfassent à ces prescriptions.

2 Compte dûment tenu de ses conditions particulières et de ses moyens, chaque Partie élabore des politiques, stratégies ou programmes nationaux pour la gestion des eaux de ballast dans ses ports et les eaux relevant de sa juridiction, qui concordent avec les objectifs de la présente Convention et en favorisent la réalisation.

Article 5
Installations de réception des sédiments

1   Chaque Partie s'engage à assurer la mise en place d'installations de réception adéquates des sédiments dans les ports et dans les terminaux qu'elle a désignés et où ont lieu le nettoyage ou les réparations des citernes à ballast, compte tenu des directives élaborées par l'Organisation. Elle veille à ce que ces installations de réception soient exploitées sans imposer de retard indu aux navires et permettent d'évacuer en toute sécurité les sédiments sans porter atteinte ni nuire à son environnement, à la santé humaine, aux biens ou aux ressources, ou à ceux d'autres États.

2   Chaque Partie notifie à l'Organisation, pour communication aux autres Parties intéressées, tous les cas où il est allégué que les installations visées au paragraphe 1 sont inadéquates.

Article 6
Recherche scientifique et technique et surveillance

1   Les Parties s'efforcent, individuellement ou collectivement, de :

    a)   promouvoir et faciliter la recherche scientifique et technique en matière de gestion des eaux de ballast; et

    b)   surveiller les effets de la gestion des eaux de ballast dans les eaux relevant de leur juridiction.

Ces activités de recherche et de surveillance devraient consister à observer, mesurer, échantillonner, évaluer et analyser l'efficacité et les impacts défavorables de toute technologie ou méthode ainsi que les impacts défavorables causés par les organismes et agents pathogènes qui ont été identifiés comme ayant été transférés par les eaux de ballast des navires.

2   Pour promouvoir les objectifs de la présente Convention, chaque Partie facilite l'accès des autres Parties qui en font la demande aux renseignements pertinents sur :

    a)   les mesures techniques et les programmes scientifiques et technologiques entrepris dans le domaine de la gestion des eaux de ballast; et

    b)   l'efficacité de la gestion des eaux de ballast, telle qu'observée lors des programmes de surveillance et d'évaluation.

Article 7
Visites et délivrance des certificats

1   Chaque Partie veille à ce que les navires autorisés à battre son pavillon ou exploités sous son autorité, qui sont soumis aux dispositions en matière de visites et de délivrance des certificats, fassent l'objet de visites et que des certificats leur soient délivrés conformément aux règles de l'Annexe.

2   Une Partie qui introduit des mesures en application de l'article 2.3 ou de la section C de l'Annexe ne doit pas exiger une visite et un certificat supplémentaires dans le cas d'un navire d'une autre Partie, et l'Administration dont relève ce navire n'est pas tenu de le soumettre à une visite et de certifier qu'il satisfait aux mesures supplémentaires imposées par une autre Partie. La Partie qui applique de telles mesures supplémentaires est responsable du contrôle de leur application qui ne doit pas causer de retard indu au navire.

Article 8
Infractions

1   Toute infraction aux prescriptions de la présente Convention est interdite et sanctionnée par la législation de l'Administration dont relève le navire en cause, où qu'elle soit commise. Si l'Administration est informée d'une telle infraction, elle effectue une enquête et peut demander à la Partie qui l'a informée de lui fournir des preuves supplémentaires de l'infraction alléguée. Si l'Administration est convaincue qu'il existe des preuves suffisantes pour permettre d'engager des poursuites au titre de l'infraction alléguée, elle fait en sorte que ces poursuites soient engagées le plus tôt possible conformément à sa législation. L'Administration informe rapidement la Partie qui a signalé l'infraction alléguée, ainsi que l'Organisation, des mesures prises. Si l'Administration n'a pris aucune mesure dans un délai de un an à compter de la réception des renseignements, elle en informe la Partie qui a signalé l'infraction alléguée.

2   Toute infraction aux prescriptions de la présente Convention commise dans la juridiction d'une Partie est interdite et sanctionnée par la législation de cette Partie. Chaque fois qu'une telle infraction se produit, la Partie doit :

a)   faire en sorte que des poursuites soient engagées conformément à sa législation; ou

b)   fournir à l'Administration dont relève le navire en cause les informations et les preuves qu'elle pourrait détenir attestant qu'il y a eu infraction.

3   Les sanctions prévues par la législation d'une Partie en application du présent article doivent être, par leur rigueur, de nature à décourager les infractions à la présente Convention où qu'elles soient commises.

Article 9
Inspection des navires

1   Un navire auquel s'applique la présente Convention peut, dans tout port ou terminal au large d'une autre Partie, être inspecté par des agents dûment autorisés par cette Partie, aux fins de déterminer s'il satisfait à la présente Convention. Sous réserve des dispositions du paragraphe 2 du présent article, une inspection de ce type se limite à :

a)   vérifier que le navire a à bord un certificat valable qui, dans ce cas, doit être accepté; et

b)   inspecter le registre des eaux de ballast; et/ou

c)   prélever des échantillons de l'eau de ballast du navire conformément aux directives élaborées par l'Organisation. Toutefois, le délai requis pour analyser ces échantillons ne doit pas être invoqué pour retarder indûment l'exploitation, le mouvement ou le départ du navire.

2   Si le navire n'est pas muni d'un certificat valable ou s'il existe de bonnes raisons de penser que :

a) l'état du navire ou de son équipement ne correspond pas en substance aux indications du certificat; ou que

b) le capitaine ou l'équipage n'est pas familiarisé avec les procédures de bord essentielles concernant la gestion des eaux de ballast ou ne les a pas appliquées,

une inspection approfondie peut être effectuée.

3   Dans les cas prévus au paragraphe 2 du présent article, la Partie qui effectue l'inspection prend les mesures nécessaires pour empêcher le navire de rejeter de l'eau de ballast jusqu'à ce qu'il puisse le faire sans présenter de menace pour l'environnement, la santé humaine, les biens ou les ressources.

Article 10
Recherche des infractions et contrôle des navires

1   Les Parties coopèrent à la recherche des infractions et à la mise en application des dispositions de la présente Convention.

2   S'il est constaté qu'un navire a enfreint la présente Convention, la Partie dont le navire est autorisé à battre le pavillon et/ou la Partie dont un port ou terminal au large est utilisé par le navire peuvent, en plus des sanctions visées à l'article 8 ou des mesures visées à l'article 9, prendre des dispositions pour mettre en garde le navire, le retenir ou ne pas l'admettre dans leurs ports. La Partie dont un port ou terminal au large est utilisé par le navire peut toutefois donner à un tel navire l'autorisation de quitter ce port ou terminal au large pour rejeter l'eau de ballast ou pour se rendre à l'installation de réception ou au chantier de réparation approprié le plus proche disponible, à condition que cela ne présente pas de menace pour l'environnement, la santé humaine, les biens ou les ressources.

3   Si les résultats de l'échantillonnage visé à l'article 9.1 c) indiquent que le navire présente une menace pour l'environnement, la santé humaine, les biens ou les ressources ou confirment les renseignements reçus d'un autre port ou terminal au large, la Partie dans les eaux de laquelle le navire est exploité interdit à ce navire de rejeter l'eau de ballast tant que la menace n'a pas été éliminée.

4   Une Partie peut aussi inspecter un navire qui entre dans un port ou un terminal au large relevant de sa juridiction si une autre Partie lui demande de procéder à une enquête en fournissant des preuves suffisantes attestant que le navire est exploité ou a été exploité en violation d'une disposition de la présente Convention. Le rapport de cette enquête est adressé à la Partie qui l'a demandée, ainsi qu'à l'autorité compétente de l'Administration dont relève le navire en cause, afin que des mesures appropriées puissent être prises.

Article 11
Notification des mesures de contrôle

1   S'il ressort d'une inspection effectuée en application de l'article 9 ou 10 qu'une infraction à la présente Convention a été commise, le navire doit en être informé. Un rapport doit être adressé à l'Administration, y compris toute preuve de l'infraction.

2   Si des mesures sont prises en application de l'article 9.3, 10.2 ou 10.3, le fonctionnaire qui prend les mesures informe immédiatement, par écrit, l'Administration dont relève le navire en cause ou, si cela n'est pas possible, le consul ou le représentant diplomatique dont dépend le navire en cause, de toutes les circonstances qui ont fait que ces mesures ont été jugées né-cessaires. L'organisme reconnu qui est responsable de la délivrance des certificats doit également en être informé.

3   L'autorité concernée de l'État du port informe, outre les Parties mentionnées au paragraphe 2, le port d'escale suivant de tous les éléments pertinents concernant l'infraction, si elle ne peut pas prendre les mesures spécifiées à l'article 9.3, 10.2 ou 10.3 ou si le navire a été autorisé à se rendre au port d'escale suivant.

Article 12
Retard causé indûment aux navires

1   Il convient d'éviter, dans toute la mesure du possible, qu'un navire soit indûment retenu ou retardé par suite de l'application de l'article 7.2, 8, 9 ou 10.

2   Un navire qui a été indûment retenu ou retardé par suite de l'ap-plication de l'article 7.2, 8, 9 ou 10 a droit à réparation pour tout préjudice ou dommage subi.

Article 13
Assistance et coopération techniques
et coopération régionale

1   Les Parties s'engagent, directement ou par l'intermédiaire de l'Orga-nisation et d'autres organismes internationaux, le cas échéant, à fournir, au titre du contrôle et de la gestion des eaux de ballast et sédiments des navires, un appui aux Parties qui demandent une assistance technique pour :

>   **a)**   former du personnel;

>   **b)**   assurer la disponibilité de technologies, de matériel et d'installa-tions appropriés;

>   **c)**   mettre en train des programmes communs de recherche-développement; et

>   **d)**   prendre d'autres mesures pour la mise en oeuvre effective de la présente Convention et des directives y relatives élaborées par l'Organisation.

2   Les Parties s'engagent à coopérer activement, sous réserve de leurs législation, réglementation et politique nationales, au transfert de technologie en matière de contrôle et de gestion des eaux de ballast et sédiments des navires.

3   Afin de promouvoir les objectifs de la présente Convention, les Parties ayant un intérêt commun à protéger l'environnement, la santé humaine, les biens et les ressources d'une région géographique donnée et, en particulier, les Parties riveraines de mers fermées ou semi-fermées, s'efforcent, compte tenu des caractéristiques régionales, de renforcer la coopération régionale, notamment en concluant des accords régionaux compatibles avec la présente Convention. Les Parties s'efforcent de coopérer avec les Parties à des accords régionaux en vue d'élaborer des procédures harmonisées.

Article 14
Communication de renseignements

1   Chaque Partie fournit à l'Organisation et, selon qu'il convient, communique à d'autres Parties les renseignements suivants :

a)   toutes prescriptions et procédures relatives à la gestion des eaux de ballast, notamment ses lois, règlements et directives pour l'application de la présente Convention;

b)   la disponibilité et l'emplacement des installations de réception pour l'évacuation des eaux de ballast et des sédiments sans danger pour l'environnement; et

c)   toutes prescriptions concernant les renseignements requis des navires qui ne peuvent pas satisfaire aux dispositions de la présente Convention pour les raisons spécifiées aux règles A-3 et B-4 de l'Annexe.

2   L'Organisation informe les Parties de toute communication reçue en vertu du présent article et diffuse à toutes les Parties les renseignements qui lui ont été communiqués en vertu des alinéas 1 b) et c) du présent article.

Article 15
Règlement des différends

Les Parties règlent tout différend survenant entre elles quant à l'interprétation ou l'application de la présente Convention par voie de négociation, d'enquête, de médiation, de conciliation, d'arbitrage, de règlement judiciaire, de recours à des organismes ou accords régionaux, ou par d'autres moyens pacifiques de leur choix.

Article 16
Rapport avec le droit international et d'autres accords

Aucune disposition de la présente Convention ne porte atteinte aux droits et obligations qu'a tout État en vertu du droit international coutumier, tel que défini dans la Convention des Nations Unies sur le droit de la mer.

Article 17
*Signature, ratification, acceptation, approbation
et adhésion*

1   La présente Convention est ouverte à la signature de tout État, au Siège de l'Organisation, du 1er juin 2004 au 31 mai 2005 et reste ensuite ouverte à l'adhésion.

2   Les États peuvent devenir Parties à la Convention par :

a)   signature sans réserve quant à la ratification, l'acceptation ou l'approbation; ou

b)   signature sous réserve de ratification, d'acceptation ou d'approbation, suivie de ratification, d'acceptation ou d'approbation; ou

c)   adhésion.

3   La ratification, l'acceptation, l'approbation ou l'adhésion s'effectue par le dépôt d'un instrument à cet effet auprès du Secrétaire général.

4   Si un État comporte deux ou plusieurs unités territoriales dans lesquelles des régimes juridiques différents sont applicables pour ce qui est des questions traitées dans la présente Convention, il peut, au moment de la signature, de la ratification, de l'acceptation, de l'approbation ou de l'adhésion, déclarer que la présente Convention s'applique à l'ensemble de ses unités territoriales ou seulement à une ou plusieurs d'entre elles et il peut modifier cette déclaration en présentant une autre déclaration à tout moment.

5   Toute déclaration de ce type est notifiée par écrit au dépositaire et mentionne expressément l'unité ou les unités territoriales auxquelles s'applique la présente Convention.

Article 18
Entrée en vigueur

1   La présente Convention entre en vigueur douze mois après la date à laquelle au moins trente États, dont les flottes marchandes représentent au total au moins trente-cinq pour cent du tonnage brut de la flotte mondiale des navires de commerce, ont soit signé la Convention sans réserve quant à la ratification, l'acceptation ou l'approbation, soit déposé l'instrument requis de ratification, d'acceptation, d'approbation ou d'adhésion, conformément à l'article 17.

2   Pour les États qui ont déposé un instrument de ratification, d'acceptation ou d'approbation de la présente Convention ou d'adhésion à celle-ci après que les conditions régissant son entrée en vigueur ont été remplies mais avant son entrée en vigueur, la ratification, l'acceptation, l'approbation ou l'adhésion prend effet à la date de l'entrée en vigueur de la présente Convention, ou trois mois après la date du dépôt de l'instrument si cette dernière date est postérieure.

3 Tout instrument de ratification, d'acceptation, d'approbation ou d'adhésion déposé après la date d'entrée en vigueur de la présente Convention prend effet trois mois après la date du dépôt de l'instrument.

4 Tout instrument de ratification, d'acceptation, d'approbation ou d'adhésion déposé après la date à laquelle un amendement à la présente Convention est réputé avoir été accepté en vertu de l'article 19 s'applique à la présente Convention telle que modifiée.

Article 19
Amendements

1 La présente Convention peut être modifiée selon l'une des procédures définies dans les paragraphes ci-après.

2 Amendements après examen au sein de l'Organisation :

a) Toute Partie peut proposer un amendement à la présente Convention. L'amendement proposé est soumis au Secrétaire général qui le diffuse aux Parties et aux Membres de l'Organisation six mois au moins avant son examen.

b) Un amendement proposé et diffusé de la manière prévue ci-dessus est renvoyé au Comité pour examen. Les Parties, qu'elles soient ou non Membres de l'Organisation, sont autorisées à participer aux délibérations du Comité aux fins de l'examen et de l'adoption de l'amendement.

c) Les amendements sont adoptés à la majorité des deux tiers des Parties présentes et votantes au sein du Comité, à condition qu'un tiers au moins des Parties soient présentes au moment du vote.

d) Les amendements adoptés conformément à l'alinéa c) sont communiqués par le Secrétaire général aux Parties pour acceptation.

e) Un amendement est réputé avoir été accepté dans les cas suivants :

    i) Un amendement à un article de la présente Convention est réputé avoir été accepté à la date à laquelle deux tiers des Parties ont notifié leur acceptation au Secrétaire général.

    ii) Un amendement à une Annexe est réputé avoir été accepté à l'expiration d'une période de douze mois après la date de son adoption ou toute autre date fixée par le Comité. Toutefois, si à cette date plus d'un tiers des Parties ont notifié au Secrétaire général qu'elles élèvent une objection contre cet amendement, celui-ci est réputé ne pas avoir été accepté.

f) Un amendement entre en vigueur dans les conditions suivantes :

    i) Un amendement à un article de la présente Convention entre en vigueur à l'égard des Parties qui ont déclaré l'avoir accepté six mois après la date à laquelle il est réputé avoir été accepté conformément à l'alinéa e) i).

    ii) Un amendement à l'Annexe entre en vigueur à l'égard de toutes les Parties six mois après la date à laquelle il est réputé avoir été accepté, à l'exception de toute Partie qui a :

        1) notifié son objection à l'amendement conformément à l'alinéa e) ii) et n'a pas retiré cette objection; ou

        2) notifié au Secrétaire général, avant l'entrée en vigueur de cet amendement, que celui-ci entrera en vigueur à son égard uniquement après notification ultérieure de son acceptation.

g) i) Une Partie qui a notifié une objection en vertu de l'alinéa f) ii) 1) peut par la suite notifier au Secrétaire général qu'elle accepte l'amendement. Cet amendement entre en vigueur pour cette Partie six mois après la date de la notification de son acceptation, ou la date d'entrée en vigueur de l'amendement, si cette dernière date est postérieure.

    ii) Si une Partie qui a adressé une notification visée à l'alinéa f) ii) 2) notifie au Secrétaire général qu'elle accepte un amendement, cet amendement entre en vigueur à l'égard de cette Partie six mois après la date de la notification de son acceptation, ou la date d'entrée en vigueur de l'amendement, si cette dernière date est postérieure.

3 Amendement par une conférence :

a) À la demande d'une Partie, appuyée par un tiers au moins des Parties, l'Organisation convoque une conférence des Parties pour examiner des amendements à la présente Convention.

b) Un amendement adopté par cette conférence à la majorité des deux tiers des Parties présentes et votantes est communiqué par le Secrétaire général à toutes les Parties pour acceptation.

c) À moins que la Conférence n'en décide autrement, l'amendement est réputé avoir été accepté et entre en vigueur conformément aux procédures définies aux alinéas 2 e) et f) respectivement.

4 Toute Partie qui n'a pas accepté un amendement à l'Annexe est considérée comme non Partie aux seules fins de l'application de cet amendement.

5 Toute notification en vertu du présent article est adressée par écrit au Secrétaire général.

6 Le Secrétaire général informe les Parties et les Membres de l'Organisation :

    a) de tout amendement qui entre en vigueur et de la date de son entrée en vigueur en général et à l'égard de chaque Partie; et

    b) de toute notification faite en vertu du présent article.

Article 20
Dénonciation

1   La présente Convention peut être dénoncée par l'une quelconque des Parties à tout moment après l'expiration d'une période de deux ans à compter de la date à laquelle elle entre en vigueur à l'égard de cette Partie.

2   La dénonciation s'effectue au moyen d'une notification écrite adressée au dépositaire et prend effet un an après la date à laquelle le dépositaire en a reçu notification ou à l'expiration de tout autre délai plus long spécifié dans la notification.

Article 21
Dépositaire

1   La présente Convention est déposée auprès du Secrétaire général, qui en adresse des copies certifiées conformes à tous les États qui l'ont signée ou qui y ont adhéré.

2   Outre les fonctions spécifiées dans d'autres dispositions de la présente Convention, le Secrétaire général :

a)   informe tous les États qui ont signé la présente Convention ou qui y ont adhéré :

  i)   de toute nouvelle signature ou de tout dépôt d'un nouvel instrument de ratification, d'acceptation, d'approbation ou d'adhésion, ainsi que de leur date;

  ii) de la date d'entrée en vigueur de la présente Convention; et

  iii) du dépôt de tout instrument de dénonciation de la Convention, ainsi que de la date à laquelle il a été reçu et de la date à laquelle la dénonciation prend effet; et

b)   dès l'entrée en vigueur de la présente Convention, en transmet le texte au Secrétariat de l'Organisation des Nations Unies en vue de son enregistrement et de sa publication conformément à l'Article 102 de la Charte des Nations Unies.

Article 22
Langues

La présente Convention est établie en un seul exemplaire original en langues anglaise, arabe, chinoise, espagnole, française et russe, chaque texte faisant également foi.

FAIT À LONDRES, ce treize février deux mille quatre.

EN FOI DE QUOI, les soussignés[*], dûment autorisés à cet effet par leurs gouvernements respectifs, ont signé la présente Convention.

---

[*] La liste des signatures n'est pas reproduite.

Annexe
Règles pour le contrôle et la gestion des eaux de ballast et sédiments des navires

SECTION A – DISPOSITIONS GÉNÉRALES

Règle A-1
Définitions

Aux fins de la présente Annexe :

1   *Date anniversaire* désigne le jour et le mois de chaque année correspondant à la date d'expiration du Certificat.

2   *Capacité en eaux de ballast* désigne la capacité volumétrique totale des citernes, espaces ou compartiments utilisés à bord d'un navire pour transporter, charger ou décharger des eaux de ballast, y compris les citernes, espaces ou compartiments polyvalents conçus pour permettre le transport d'eaux de ballast.

3   *Compagnie* désigne le propriétaire du navire ou tout autre organisme ou personne, telle que l'armateur gérant ou l'affréteur coque nue, auquel le propriétaire du navire a confié la responsabilité de l'exploitation du navire et qui, en assumant cette responsabilité, s'acquitte des tâches et des obligations imposées par le Code international de gestion de la sécurité*.

4   *Construit*, s'agissant d'un navire, désigne le stade auquel :

   .1   la quille est posée; ou

   .2   une construction identifiable au navire particulier commence; ou

   .3   le montage du navire considéré a commencé, employant au moins 50 tonnes ou 1 pour cent de la masse estimée de tous les matériaux de construction, si cette dernière valeur est inférieure; ou

   .4   le navire subit une transformation importante.

5   *Transformation importante* désigne une transformation :

   .1   qui modifie la capacité en eaux de ballast d'un navire de 15 % ou plus; ou

   .2   qui change le type du navire; ou

   .3   qui vise, de l'avis de l'Administration, à prolonger la vie d'un navire de 10 ans ou plus; ou

---

*   Il convient de se reporter au Code ISM que l'Organisation a adopté par la résolution A.741(18), telle que modifiée.

.4 qui entraîne des modifications du système d'eaux de ballast d'un navire autres que le remplacement des éléments. La transformation d'un navire pour répondre aux dispositions de la règle D-1 ne doit pas être considérée comme constituant une transformation importante aux fins de la présente Annexe.

6 *À partir de la terre la plus proche* signifie à partir de la ligne de base qui sert à déterminer la mer territoriale du territoire en question conformément au droit international; toutefois, aux fins de la Convention, l'expression «à partir de la terre la plus proche» de la côte nord-est de l'Australie signifie à partir d'une ligne reliant le point de latitude 11°00'S et de longitude 142°08'E sur la côte australienne et le point de latitude 10°35'S et de longitude 141°55'E, puis les points suivants :

latitude 10°00'S et longitude 142°00'E
latitude 9°10'S et longitude 143°52'E
latitude 9°00'S et longitude 144°30'E
latitude 10°41'S et longitude 145°00'E
latitude 13°00'S et longitude 145°00'E
latitude 15°00'S et longitude 146°00'E
latitude 17°30'S et longitude 147°00'E
latitude 21°00'S et longitude 152°55'E
latitude 24°30'S et longitude 154°00'E
et enfin le point de latitude 24°42'S
et de longitude 153°15'E sur la côte australienne.

7 *Substance active* désigne une substance ou un organisme, y compris un virus ou un champignon, qui agit de manière générale ou spécifique sur ou contre des organismes aquatiques nuisibles et des agents pathogènes.

Règle A-2
Applicabilité générale

Sauf disposition expresse contraire, le rejet des eaux de ballast ne doit être effectué qu'au moyen de la gestion des eaux de ballast conformément aux dispositions de la présente Annexe.

Règle A-3
Exceptions

Les prescriptions de la règle B-3, ou les mesures éventuellement adoptées par une Partie conformément aux dispositions de l'article 2.3 ou de la section C, ne s'appliquent pas :

.1 à la prise ou au rejet d'eaux de ballast et de sédiments nécessaire pour garantir la sécurité d'un navire dans des situations d'urgence ou la sauvegarde de la vie humaine en mer; ou

.2 au rejet accidentel ou à l'entrée d'eaux de ballast et de sédiments résultant d'une avarie survenue au navire ou à son équipement :

.1 à condition que toutes les précautions raisonnables aient été prises avant et après la survenance de l'avarie ou la découverte de l'avarie ou du rejet pour empêcher ou réduire au minimum ce rejet; et

.2   à moins que l'avarie ne soit due à un acte délibéré ou téméraire du propriétaire, de la compagnie ou de l'officier ayant la charge du navire;

.3   à la prise et au rejet d'eaux de ballast et de sédiments lorsque ces opérations ont pour but d'éviter ou de réduire au minimum un événement de pollution par le navire; ou

.4   à la prise et au rejet ultérieur en haute mer des mêmes eaux de ballast et sédiments ou;

.5   au rejet d'eaux de ballast et de sédiments par un navire, sur le lieu même d'origine de la totalité des eaux de ballast et sédiments et à condition qu'il n'y ait pas de mélange avec des eaux de ballast non gérées et des sédiments provenant d'autres zones. Si un mélange s'est produit, les eaux de ballast provenant d'autres zones sont soumises à la gestion des eaux de ballast conformément à la présente Annexe.

Règle A-4
Exemptions

1   Outre les exemptions prévues dans d'autres dispositions de la présente Convention, Une Partie ou des Parties peuvent, dans les eaux relevant de leur juridiction, accorder des dispenses de toute obligation d'appliquer la règle B-3 ou C-1, mais uniquement lorsque ces dispenses sont :

.1   accordées à un ou plusieurs navires effectuant une ou plusieurs traversées entre des ports ou lieux spécifiés; ou à un navire exploité exclusivement entre des ports ou lieux spécifiés;

.2   valables pour une période ne dépassant pas cinq ans, sous réserve d'un examen dans l'intervalle;

.3   accordées à des navires qui ne mélangent pas d'eaux de ballast et de sédiments autres que ceux provenant des ports ou lieux spécifiés au paragraphe 1.1; et

.4   accordées conformément aux directives sur l'évaluation des risques élaborées par l'Organisation.

2   Les dispenses accordées en application du paragraphe 1 ne doivent pas prendre effet avant d'avoir été communiquées à l'Organisation et avant que les renseignements pertinents aient été diffusés aux Parties.

3   Aucune dispense accordée en vertu de la présente règle ne doit porter atteinte ou nuire à l'environnement, à la santé humaine, aux biens ou aux ressources d'États adjacents ou d'autres États. Si la Partie établit qu'une dispense peut causer un préjudice à un État, celui-ci doit être consulté dans le but de résoudre tout problème identifié.

4   Toute dispense accordée en vertu de la présente règle doit être consignée dans le registre des eaux de ballast.

Règle A-5
Respect de conditions équivalentes

Le respect de conditions équivalentes à celles de la présente Annexe pour les engins de plaisance utilisés exclusivement à des fins récréatives ou sportives ou les engins utilisés essentiellement aux fins de la recherche et du sauvetage, d'une longueur hors tout inférieure à 50 mètres et d'une capacité maximale en eaux de ballast de 8 mètres cubes, est établi par l'Administration compte tenu des directives élaborées par l'Organisation.

SECTION B – PRESCRIPTIONS EN MATIÈRE DE GESTION ET DE CONTRÔLE APPLICABLES AUX NAVIRES

Règle B-1
Plan de gestion des eaux de ballast

Chaque navire doit avoir à bord et mettre en oeuvre un plan de gestion des eaux de ballast. Ce plan doit être approuvé par l'Administration compte tenu des directives élaborées par l'Organisation. Le plan de gestion des eaux de ballast doit être spécifique à chaque navire et doit au moins :

.1 décrire en détail les procédures de sécurité que le navire et l'équipage doivent suivre pour la gestion des eaux de ballast conformément à la présente Convention;

.2 fournir une description détaillée des mesures à prendre pour mettre en oeuvre les prescriptions relatives à la gestion des eaux de ballast et les pratiques complémentaires de gestion des eaux de ballast qui sont énoncées dans la présente Convention;

.3 décrire en détail les procédures d'évacuation des sédiments :

.1 en mer; et

.2 à terre;

.4 décrire les procédures de coordination de la gestion des eaux de ballast à bord qui impliquent le rejet en mer, avec les autorités de l'État dans les eaux duquel ce rejet sera effectué;

.5 désigner l'officier de bord chargé d'assurer la mise en oeuvre correcte du plan;

.6 contenir les prescriptions en matière de notification applicables aux navires en vertu de la présente Convention; et

.7 être rédigé dans la langue de travail du navire. Si la langue utilisée n'est ni l'anglais, ni l'espagnol, ni le français, le plan doit comprendre une traduction dans l'une de ces langues.

Règle B-2
Registre des eaux de ballast

1   Chaque navire doit avoir à bord un registre des eaux de ballast qui peut être sur support électronique ou faire partie d'un autre registre ou système d'enregistrement et qui doit contenir au moins les renseignements spécifiés à l'appendice II.

2   Les mentions portées sur le registre des eaux de ballast doivent être conservées à bord pendant une période minimale de deux ans à compter de la dernière inscription, puis sous le contrôle de la compagnie pendant une période minimale de trois ans.

3   En cas de rejet d'eaux de ballast effectué en conformité avec la règle A-3, A-4 ou B-3.6, ou en cas d'autre rejet accidentel ou exceptionnel qui ne fait pas l'objet des exemptions prévues par la présente Convention, les circonstances et les motifs du rejet doivent être indiqués dans le registre des eaux de ballast.

4   Le registre des eaux de ballast doit être conservé de manière à être aisément accessible aux fins d'inspection à tout moment raisonnable et, dans le cas d'un navire remorqué sans équipage, peut se trouver à bord du navire remorqueur.

5   Chacune des opérations concernant la gestion des eaux de ballast doit être intégralement et dès que possible consignée dans le registre des eaux de ballast. Chaque mention doit être signée par l'officier responsable de l'opé-ration en question et chaque page, lorsqu'elle est terminée, doit être signée par le capitaine. Les mentions doivent être consignées dans une langue de travail du navire. Si cette langue n'est ni l'anglais, ni l'espagnol, ni le français, ces mentions doivent comporter une traduction dans l'une de ces langues. En cas de différend ou de divergence, les mentions écrites dans une langue officielle de l'État dont le navire est autorisé à battre le pavillon font foi.

6   Les agents dûment autorisés par une Partie peuvent inspecter le re-gistre des eaux de ballast à bord de tout navire auquel s'applique la présente règle pendant qu'il se trouve dans un de ses ports ou terminaux au large. Ils peuvent en extraire des copies et en exiger la certification par le capitaine. Toute copie ainsi certifiée est, en cas de poursuites, admissible en justice comme preuve des faits relatés dans le registre. L'inspection du registre des eaux de ballast et l'établissement de copies certifiées doivent être effectués de la façon la plus prompte possible et sans que le navire ne soit indûment retardé.

Règle B-3
Gestion des eaux de ballast par les navires

1   Un navire construit avant 2009 :

.1   qui a une capacité en eaux de ballast comprise entre 1 500 et 5 000 mètres cubes inclus, doit procéder à la gestion des eaux de ballast de façon à satisfaire au moins à la norme décrite à la règle D-1 ou à la règle D-2 jusqu'en 2014, date après laquelle il doit satisfaire au moins à la norme décrite à la règle D-2;

.2 qui a une capacité en eaux de ballast inférieure à 1 500 ou supérieure à 5 000 mètres cubes doit procéder à la gestion des eaux de ballast de façon à satisfaire au moins à la norme décrite à la règle D-1 ou à la règle D-2 jusqu'en 2016, date après laquelle il doit satisfaire au moins à la norme décrite à la règle D-2.

2   Un navire auquel s'applique le paragraphe 1 doit satisfaire à ses dispositions au plus tard à la date de la première visite intermédiaire ou de renouvellement, selon celle qui intervient en premier, après la date anniversaire de la livraison du navire l'année où la norme applicable au navire doit être respectée.

3   Un navire construit en 2009 ou après cette date qui a une capacité en eaux de ballast inférieure à 5 000 mètres cubes doit procéder à la gestion des eaux de ballast de façon à satisfaire au moins à la norme décrite à la règle D-2.

4   Un navire construit en 2009 ou après cette date, mais avant 2012, qui a une capacité en eaux de ballast égale ou supérieure à 5 000 mètres cubes doit procéder à la gestion des eaux de ballast conformément au paragraphe 1.2.

5   Un navire construit en 2012 ou après cette date qui a une capacité en eaux de ballast égale ou supérieure à 5 000 mètres cubes doit procéder à la gestion des eaux de ballast de façon à satisfaire au moins à la norme décrite à la règle D-2.

6   Les prescriptions de la présente règle ne s'appliquent pas aux navires qui rejettent des eaux de ballast dans une installation de réception conçue compte tenu des directives élaborées par l'Organisation pour de telles installations.

7   D'autres méthodes de gestion des eaux de ballast peuvent également être acceptées en remplacement des prescriptions énoncées aux paragraphes 1 à 5, sous réserve qu'elles assurent au moins le même degré de protection de l'environnement, de la santé humaine, des biens ou des ressources, et qu'elles soient approuvées en principe par le Comité.

Règle B-4
Renouvellement des eaux de ballast

1   Un navire qui procède au renouvellement des eaux de ballast pour satisfaire à la norme de la règle D.1 doit :

.1 autant que possible, effectuer le renouvellement des eaux de ballast à 200 milles marins au moins de la terre la plus proche et par 200 mètres de fond au moins, compte tenu des directives élaborées par l'Organisation;

.2 lorsque le navire n'est pas en mesure de procéder au renouvellement des eaux de ballast conformément au paragraphe 1.1, ce renouvellement du ballast doit être effectué compte tenu des directives visées au paragraphe 1.1 et aussi loin que possible de la terre la plus proche et, dans tous les cas, à une distance d'au moins 50 milles marins de la terre la plus proche et par 200 mètres de fond au moins.

2   Dans les zones maritimes où la distance de la terre la plus proche ou la profondeur ne répond pas aux paramètres visés au paragraphe 1.1 ou 1.2, l'État du port peut désigner, en consultation avec les États adjacents ou d'autres États, selon qu'il convient, des zones où un navire peut procéder au renouvellement des eaux de ballast compte tenu des directives visées au paragraphe 1.1.

3   Un navire n'est pas tenu de s'écarter de la route prévue ou de retarder son voyage pour satisfaire à une prescription particulière du paragraphe 1.

4   Un navire qui procède au renouvellement des eaux de ballast n'est pas tenu de satisfaire aux dispositions du paragraphe 1 ou 2, selon le cas, si le capitaine décide raisonnablement qu'une telle opération compromettrait la stabilité ou la sécurité du navire, de son équipage ou de ses passagers du fait de conditions météorologiques défavorables, de la conception du navire ou des efforts auxquels il est soumis, d'une défaillance de l'équipement ou de toute autre circonstance exceptionnelle.

5   Lorsqu'un navire est tenu de procéder au renouvellement des eaux de ballast et ne le fait pas conformément à la présente règle, les raisons doivent être consignées sur le registre des eaux de ballast.

Règle B-5
Gestion des sédiments par les navires

1   Tous les navires doivent éliminer et évacuer les sédiments des espaces destinés aux eaux de ballast conformément aux dispositions du plan de gestion des eaux de ballast du navire.

2   Les navires visés à la règle B-3.3 à B-3.5 devraient, sans que cela porte atteinte à la sécurité ou à l'efficacité de l'exploitation, être conçus et construits de manière à réduire au minimum la prise et la rétention indésirable de sédiments, à faciliter l'élimination des sédiments et à permettre un accès sans danger pour procéder à l'élimination et l'échantillonnage des sédiments, compte tenu des directives élaborées par l'Organisation. Les navires visés à la règle B-3.1 devraient, dans la mesure où cela est possible dans la pratique, satisfaire aux dispositions du présent paragraphe.

Règle B-6
Tâches des officiers et des membres d'équipage

Les officiers et les membres d'équipage doivent être familiarisés avec les tâches afférentes à la gestion des eaux de ballast spécifique au navire à bord duquel ils servent et doivent, en fonction des tâches qui leur sont assignées, être familiarisés avec le plan de gestion des eaux de ballast du navire.

SECTION C – PRESCRIPTIONS SPÉCIALES DANS CERTAINES ZONES

Règle C-1
Mesures supplémentaires

1   Si une Partie, individuellement ou de concert avec d'autres Parties, décide que des mesures supplémentaires à celles de la section B sont nécessaires pour prévenir, réduire ou éliminer le transfert d'organismes aquatiques nuisibles et d'agents pathogènes par les eaux de ballast et sédiments des navires, cette ou ces Parties peuvent, conformément au droit international, exiger que les navires satisfassent à une norme ou prescription spécifiée.

2   Avant d'établir des normes ou prescriptions conformément au paragraphe 1, la ou les Parties devraient consulter les États adjacents ou d'autres États susceptibles d'être affectés par de telles normes ou prescriptions.

3   La ou les Parties qui ont l'intention d'introduire des mesures supplémentaires conformément au paragraphe 1 de la présente règle doivent :

> **.1**   tenir compte des directives élaborées par l'Organisation;
>
> **.2**   informer l'Organisation de leur intention d'établir des mesures supplémentaires au moins 6 mois avant la date prévue de mise en oeuvre desdites mesures, sauf en cas d'urgence ou d'épidémie. La notification doit indiquer :
>
>> **.1**   les coordonnées géographiques exactes des lieux où ces mesures supplémentaires s'appliquent;
>>
>> **.2**   la nécessité et la justification de l'application des mesures supplémentaires, y compris, si possible, les avantages de ces mesures;
>>
>> **.3**   une description des mesures supplémentaires; et
>>
>> **.4**   tout arrangement éventuellement prévu pour faciliter le respect par les navires des mesures supplémentaires;
>
> **.3**   dans la mesure requise par le droit international coutumier, tel que défini dans la Convention des Nations Unies sur le droit de la mer, obtenir l'approbation de l'Organisation.

4   La ou les Parties qui introduisent de telles mesures supplémentaires doivent s'efforcer de procurer, autant que possible, tous les services appropriés, lesquels peuvent comprendre, sans toutefois s'y limiter, des avis aux navigateurs concernant les zones, les autres itinéraires ou ports possibles, pour alléger la charge imposée au navire.

5 Les mesures supplémentaires adoptées par une ou plusieurs Parties ne doivent pas compromettre la sécurité et la sûreté du navire et ne doivent en aucun cas être en conflit avec toute autre convention à laquelle le navire serait soumis.

6 La ou les Parties qui introduisent des mesures supplémentaires peuvent renoncer à les appliquer temporairement ou dans des circonstances particulières si elles le jugent approprié.

Règle C-2
Avis concernant la prise d'eaux de ballast dans certaines zones et mesures connexes que doivent prendre les États du pavillon

1 Une Partie doit s'efforcer de diffuser des avis aux navigateurs concernant les zones relevant de leur juridiction dans lesquelles les navires ne devraient pas prendre d'eaux de ballast en raison de conditions connues. La Partie doit préciser dans ces avis les coordonnées géographiques exactes de la ou des zones susvisées et, si possible, l'emplacement d'une ou de plusieurs autres zones convenant à la prise d'eaux de ballast. Des avis peuvent être diffusés concernant :

    .1 les zones où l'on sait qu'existent des éclosions, infestations ou populations d'organismes aquatiques nuisibles ou d'agents pathogènes (par exemple, proliférations d'algues toxiques) susceptibles d'avoir une incidence sur la prise ou le rejet d'eaux de ballast;

    .2 les zones proches de points de rejet des eaux usées; ou

    .3 les zones où l'action de chasse des marées est insuffisante, ou encore les périodes pendant lesquelles on sait qu'un courant de marée cause une turbidité accrue.

2 Outre les avis diffusés aux navigateurs conformément aux dispositions du paragraphe 1, une Partie doit notifier à l'Organisation et aux États côtiers qui pourraient être affectés toute zone identifiée conformément au paragraphe 1, ainsi que la période durant laquelle l'avis restera probablement valable. La notification adressée à l'Organisation et aux États côtiers qui pourraient être affectés doit spécifier les coordonnées géographiques exactes de la zone ou des zones susmentionnées et, si possible, indiquer l'emplacement d'une ou plusieurs autres zones convenant à la prise d'eaux de ballast. L'avis doit indiquer aux navires qui ont besoin de prendre des eaux de ballast dans la zone les autres dispositions prévues à cet égard. La Partie doit également informer les gens de mer, l'Organisation et les États côtiers qui pourraient être affectés lorsqu'un avis donné n'est plus applicable.

Règle C-3
Communication de renseignements

L'Organisation doit diffuser, par tout moyen approprié, les renseignements qui lui sont communiqués en vertu des règles C-1 et C-2.

SECTION D – NORMES APPLICABLES À LA GESTION DES EAUX DE BALLAST

Règle D-1
Norme de renouvellement des eaux de ballast

1   Les navires qui procèdent au renouvellement des eaux de ballast conformément à la présente règle doivent obtenir un renouvellement volumétrique effectif d'au moins 95 pour cent des eaux de ballast.

2   Dans le cas des navires qui procèdent au renouvellement des eaux de ballast par pompage, le renouvellement par pompage de trois fois le volume de chaque citerne à ballast doit être considéré comme satisfaisant à la norme décrite au paragraphe 1. Le pompage de moins de trois fois le volume peut être accepté à condition que le navire puisse prouver qu'un renouvellement volumétrique de 95 pour cent est obtenu.

Règle D-2
Norme de qualité des eaux de ballast

1   Les navires qui procèdent à la gestion des eaux de ballast conformément à la présente règle doivent rejeter moins de 10 organismes viables par mètre cube d'une taille minimale égale ou supérieure à 50 microns et moins de 10 organismes viables par millilitre d'une taille minimale inférieure à 50 microns et supérieure à 10 microns; en outre, le rejet des agents microbiens indicateurs ne doit pas dépasser les concentrations spécifiées au paragraphe 2.

2   À titre de norme pour la santé humaine, les agents microbiens indicateurs comprennent les agents suivants :

   .1   *Vibrio cholerae* toxigène (O1 et O139), moins de 1 unité formant colonie (ufc) par 100 millilitres ou moins de 1 ufc pour 1 gramme (masse humide) d'échantillons de zooplancton;

   .2   *Escherichia coli*, moins de 250 ufc par 100 millilitres;

   .3   entérocoque intestinal, moins de 100 ufc par 100 millilitres.

Règle D-3
*Prescriptions relatives à l'approbation
des systèmes de gestion des eaux de ballast*

1   Sous réserve des dispositions du paragraphe 2, les systèmes de gestion des eaux de ballast utilisés pour satisfaire à la Convention doivent être approuvés par l'Administration compte tenu des directives élaborées par l'Organisation.

2   Les systèmes de gestion des eaux de ballast qui utilisent des substances actives ou des préparations contenant une ou plusieurs substances actives pour satisfaire à la présente Convention doivent être approuvés par l'Organisation, sur la base d'une procédure élaborée par l'Organisation. Cette procédure doit décrire l'approbation et l'annulation de l'approbation des substances actives et la manière dont il est proposé de les appliquer. À compter du retrait de l'approbation, l'utilisation de la ou des substances actives concernées doit être interdite dans l'année qui suit ce retrait.

3   Les systèmes de gestion des eaux de ballast utilisés pour satisfaire à la Convention doivent être sans danger pour le navire, son armement et l'équipage.

Règle D-4
Prototypes de technologies de traitement des eaux de ballast

1   Si, avant la date à laquelle la norme de la règle D-2 lui serait normalement applicable, un navire participe à un programme approuvé par l'Administration pour mettre à l'essai et évaluer une technologie prometteuse de traitement des eaux de ballast, la norme de la règle D-2 ne s'applique pas à ce navire avant un délai de cinq ans à compter de la date à laquelle il serait normalement tenu de la respecter.

2   Si, après la date à laquelle la norme de la règle D-2 lui devient applicable, un navire participe à un programme approuvé par l'Administration compte tenu des directives élaborées par l'Organisation, pour mettre à l'essai et évaluer une technologie prometteuse en matière d'eaux de ballast qui pourrait déboucher sur une technologie de traitement permettant de satisfaire à une norme supérieure à celle de la règle D-2, la norme de la règle D-2 ne lui est plus applicable cinq ans après la date à laquelle il est équipé de cette technologie.

3   Lorsqu'elles établissent et exécutent un programme quelconque de mise à l'essai et d'évaluation de technologies prometteuses de traitement des eaux de ballast, les Parties doivent :

   .1   tenir compte des directives élaborées par l'Organisation, et

   .2   ne faire participer que le minimum de navires nécessaire pour mettre efficacement à l'essai ces technologies.

4   Pendant toute la période d'essai et d'évaluation, le système de traitement doit être exploité régulièrement et de la façon prévue.

Règle D-5
Examen des normes par l'Organisation

1   Lors d'une réunion du Comité qui a lieu au plus tard trois ans avant la date la plus proche à laquelle la norme de la règle D-2 prendra effet, le Comité entreprend un examen pour déterminer s'il existe des technologies permettant de satisfaire à ladite norme, évaluer les critères énoncés au paragraphe 2 et analyser les effets socio-économiques compte tenu en particulier des besoins des pays en développement, et notamment ceux des petits États insulaires en développement. Le Comité doit également entreprendre des examens périodiques, selon les besoins, des prescriptions

applicables aux navires visés à la règle B-3.1 ainsi que de tout autre aspect de la gestion des eaux de ballast traité dans la présente Annexe, y compris les directives élaborées par l'Organisation.

2 Les examens en question des technologies appropriées doivent également tenir compte :

> **.1** des considérations liées à la sécurité du navire et de l'équipage;
>
> **.2** de leur acceptabilité sur le plan écologique, c'est-à-dire qu'elles ne doivent pas avoir davantage d'impacts sur l'environnement que ceux qu'elles permettent d'éviter;
>
> **.3** de leur aspect pratique, c'est-à-dire leur compatibilité avec la conception et l'exploitation du navire;
>
> **.4** de leur rapport coût-efficacité, c'est-à-dire leur caractère économique; et
>
> **.5** de leur efficacité sur le plan biologique au sens où elles permettent d'éliminer ou de rendre non viables les organismes aquatiques nuisibles et les agents pathogènes présents dans les eaux de ballast.

3 Le Comité peut constituer un ou plusieurs groupes chargés de procéder à l'examen ou aux examens visés au paragraphe 1. Le Comité arrête la composition et le mandat de tels groupes, ainsi que les questions précises qui leurs sont confiées. Ces groupes peuvent élaborer et recommander des propositions d'amendement à la présente Annexe pour examen par les Parties. Seules les Parties peuvent participer à la formulation de recommandations et aux décisions prises par le Comité à l'égard des amendements.

4 Si, sur la base des examens visés dans la présente règle, les Parties décident d'adopter des amendements à la présente Annexe, ces amendements sont adoptés et entrent en vigueur conformément aux procédures prévues à l'article 19 de la présente Convention.

SECTION E – PRESCRIPTIONS EN MATIÈRE DE VISITES ET DE DÉLIVRANCE DES CERTIFICATS AUX FINS DE LA GESTION DES EAUX DE BALLAST

Règle E-1
Visites

1 Les navires d'une jauge brute égale ou supérieure à 400 auxquels s'applique la Convention, à l'exception des plates-formes flottantes, des FSU et des FPSO, doivent être soumis aux visites spécifiées ci-après :

> **.1** Une visite initiale avant la mise en service du navire ou avant que le certificat prescrit en vertu de la règle E-2 ou E-3 ne lui soit délivré pour la première fois. Cette visite doit permettre de vérifier que le plan de gestion des eaux de ballast prescrit par la règle B-1 et la structure, l'équipement, les systèmes, les installations, les

aménagements et les matériaux ou procédés associés satisfont pleinement aux prescriptions de la présente Convention.

.2 Une visite de renouvellement effectuée aux intervalles spécifiés par l'Administration, mais n'excédant pas cinq ans, sous réserve des dispositions de la règle E-5.2, E-5.5, E-5.6 ou E-5.7. Cette visite doit permettre de vérifier que le plan de gestion des eaux de ballast prescrit par la règle B-1 et la structure, l'équipement, les systèmes, les installations, les aménagements et les matériaux ou procédés associés satisfont pleinement aux prescriptions applicables de la présente Convention.

.3 Une visite intermédiaire effectuée dans un délai de trois mois avant ou après la deuxième date anniversaire du certificat, ou dans un délai de trois mois avant ou après la troisième date anniversaire du certificat qui remplace l'une des visites annuelles prévues au paragraphe 1.4. La visite intermédiaire doit permettre de s'assurer que l'équipement et les systèmes et procédés associés de gestion des eaux de ballast satisfont pleinement aux prescriptions applicables de la présente Annexe et sont en bon état de fonctionnement. Ces visites intermédiaires doivent être portées sur le certificat délivré en vertu de la règle E-2 ou E-3.

.4 Une visite annuelle effectuée dans un délai de trois mois avant ou après chaque date anniversaire, qui comprend une inspection générale de la structure, de l'équipement, des systèmes, des installations, des aménagements et des matériaux ou procédés associés au plan de gestion des eaux de ballast prescrit par la règle B-1, afin de s'assurer qu'ils ont été maintenus dans les conditions prévues au paragraphe 9 et restent satisfaisants pour le service auquel le navire est destiné. Ces visites annuelles doivent être portées sur le certificat délivré en vertu de la règle E-2 ou E-3.

.5 Une visite supplémentaire, générale ou partielle selon le cas, qui doit être effectuée à la suite d'un changement, d'un remplacement ou d'une réparation importante de la structure, de l'équipement, des systèmes, des installations, des aménagements et des matériaux, nécessaire pour assurer la pleine conformité avec la présente Convention. Cette visite doit permettre de s'assurer que tout changement, remplacement ou toute réparation importante a été réellement effectuée de telle sorte que le navire satisfait aux prescriptions de la présente Convention. Ces visites doivent être portées sur le certificat délivré en vertu de la règle E-2 ou E-3.

2 Dans le cas des navires qui ne sont pas soumis aux dispositions du paragraphe 1, l'Administration détermine les mesures à prendre pour s'assurer que les dispositions applicables de la présente Convention sont respectées.

3 Les visites de navires aux fins de l'application des dispositions de la présente Convention doivent être effectuées par des agents de l'Administration. L'Administration peut toutefois confier les visites soit à des inspecteurs désignés à cet effet, soit à des organismes reconnus par elle.

4   Toute Administration qui désigne des inspecteurs ou des organismes reconnus pour effectuer les visites prévues au paragraphe 3 doit au moins habiliter ces inspecteurs ou organismes reconnus[*] à :

> **.1**   exiger qu'un navire soumis à une visite satisfasse aux dispositions de la présente Convention; et

> **.2**   effectuer des visites et des inspections à la requête des autorités compétentes d'un État du port qui est Partie.

5   L'Administration doit notifier à l'Organisation les responsabilités spécifiques confiées aux inspecteurs désignés ou aux organismes reconnus et les conditions de leur habilitation afin qu'elle les diffuse aux Parties pour l'information de leurs agents.

6   Lorsque l'Administration, un inspecteur désigné ou un organisme reconnu détermine que la gestion des eaux de ballast du navire ne correspond pas aux indications du certificat prescrit en vertu de la règle E-2 ou E-3 ou est telle que le navire n'est pas apte à prendre la mer sans présenter de menace pour l'environnement, la santé humaine, les biens ou les ressources, cet inspecteur ou organisme doit veiller immédiatement à ce que des mesures correctives soient prises pour rendre le navire conforme. Un inspecteur ou organisme doit être informé immédiatement et faire en sorte que le certificat ne soit pas délivré ou soit retiré, selon le cas. Si le navire se trouve dans un port d'une autre Partie, les autorités compétentes de l'État du port doivent être informées immédiatement. Lorsqu'un agent de l'Administration, un inspecteur désigné ou un organisme reconnu a informé les autorités compétentes de l'État du port, le gouvernement de l'État du port intéressé doit fournir à l'agent, à l'inspecteur ou à l'organisme en question toute l'assistance nécessaire pour lui permettre de s'acquitter de ses obligations en vertu de la présente règle, et notamment de prendre les mesures décrites à l'article 9.

7   Lorsqu'un accident survenu à un navire ou un défaut constaté à bord compromet fondamentalement l'aptitude du navire à procéder à la gestion des eaux de ballast conformément à la présente Convention, le propriétaire, l'exploitant ou toute autre personne ayant la charge du navire doit faire rapport dès que possible à l'Administration, à l'organisme reconnu ou à l'inspecteur désigné chargé de délivrer le certificat pertinent, lequel doit faire entreprendre une enquête afin de déterminer s'il est nécessaire de procéder à une visite conformément au paragraphe 1. Si le navire se trouve dans un port d'une autre Partie, le propriétaire, l'exploitant ou toute autre personne ayant la charge du navire doit également faire rapport immédiatement aux autorités compétentes de l'État du port et l'inspecteur désigné ou l'organisme reconnu doit s'assurer qu'un tel rapport a bien été fait.

8   Dans tous les cas, l'Administration intéressée se porte pleinement garante de l'exécution complète et de l'efficacité de la visite et s'engage à prendre les mesures nécessaires pour satisfaire à cette obligation.

---

[*] Se reporter aux Directives que l'Organisation a adoptées par la résolution A.739(18), telles qu'elles pourraient être modifiées par l'Organisation et aux spécifications que l'Organisation a adoptées par la résolution A.789(19), telles qu'elles pourraient être modifiées par l'Organisation.

9 L'état du navire et de son équipement, de ses systèmes et de ses procédés doit être maintenu conformément aux dispositions de la présente Convention de manière que le navire demeure à tous égards apte à prendre la mer sans présenter de menace pour l'environnement, la santé humaine, les biens ou les ressources.

10 Après l'une quelconque des visites prévues au paragraphe 1, aucun changement autre qu'un simple remplacement du matériel et des installations ne doit être apporté à la structure, à l'équipement, aux installations, aux aménagements ou aux matériaux associés au plan de gestion des eaux de ballast prescrit par la règle B-1 et ayant fait l'objet de la visite, sauf autorisation de l'Administration.

Règle E-2
Délivrance d'un certificat ou apposition d'un visa

1 L'Administration doit veiller à ce qu'un certificat soit délivré à un navire auquel s'applique la règle E-1, après l'achèvement satisfaisant d'une visite effectuée conformément à ladite règle. Un certificat délivré sous l'autorité d'une Partie à la présente Convention doit être accepté par les autres Parties et considéré, à toutes les fins visées par la présente Convention, comme ayant la même validité qu'un certificat délivré par elles.

2 Les certificats doivent être délivrés ou visés soit par l'Administration, soit par tout agent ou organisme dûment autorisé par elle. Dans tous les cas, l'Administration assume l'entière responsabilité du certificat.

Règle E-3
Délivrance d'un certificat ou apposition d'un visa par une autre Partie

1 Une autre Partie peut, à la requête de l'Administration, faire visiter un navire et, si elle estime qu'il satisfait aux dispositions de la présente Convention, elle lui délivre un certificat ou en autorise la délivrance et, le cas échéant, appose un visa ou autorise l'apposition d'un visa sur le certificat dont est muni le navire, conformément à la présente Annexe.

2 Une copie du certificat et une copie du rapport de visite doivent être adressées dès que possible à l'Administration qui a fait la requête.

3 Un certificat ainsi délivré doit comporter une déclaration établissant qu'il a été délivré à la requête de l'Administration; il a la même valeur et doit être accepté dans les mêmes conditions qu'un certificat délivré par l'Administration.

4 Il ne doit pas être délivré de certificat à un navire qui est autorisé à battre le pavillon d'un État qui n'est pas Partie.

Règle E-4
Modèle du certificat

Le certificat doit être établi dans la langue officielle de la Partie qui le délivre, selon le modèle qui figure à l'appendice I. Si la langue utilisée n'est ni l'anglais, ni l'espagnol, ni le français, le texte doit comprendre une traduction dans l'une de ces langues.

Règle E-5
Durée et validité du certificat

1   Le certificat doit être délivré pour une durée spécifiée par l'Administration, qui ne doit pas dépasser cinq ans.

2   Pour les visites de renouvellement :

.1   Nonobstant les prescriptions du paragraphe 1, lorsque la visite de renouvellement est achevée dans un délai de trois mois avant la date d'expiration du certificat existant, le nouveau certificat est valable à compter de la date d'achèvement de la visite de renouvellement jusqu'à une date qui n'est pas postérieure de plus de cinq ans à la date d'expiration du certificat existant.

.2   Lorsque la visite de renouvellement est achevée après la date d'expiration du certificat existant, le nouveau certificat est valable à compter de la date d'achèvement de la visite de renouvellement jusqu'à une date qui n'est pas postérieure de plus de cinq ans à la date d'expiration du certificat existant.

.3   Lorsque la visite de renouvellement est achevée plus de trois mois avant la date d'expiration du certificat existant, le nouveau certificat est valable à compter de la date d'achèvement de la visite de renouvellement jusqu'à une date qui n'est pas postérieure de plus de cinq ans à la date d'achèvement de la visite de renouvellement.

3   Si un certificat est délivré pour une durée inférieure à cinq ans, l'Administration peut proroger la validité dudit certificat au-delà de la date d'expiration jusqu'à concurrence de la période maximale prévue au paragraphe 1, à condition que les visites spécifiées à la règle E-1.1.3, qui doivent avoir lieu lorsqu'un certificat est délivré pour cinq ans, soient effectuées selon que de besoin.

4   Si, après une visite de renouvellement, un nouveau certificat ne peut pas être délivré ou remis au navire avant la date d'expiration du certificat existant, la personne ou l'organisme autorisé par l'Administration peut apposer un visa sur le certificat existant et ce certificat doit être accepté comme valable pour une nouvelle période qui ne peut pas dépasser cinq mois à compter de la date d'expiration.

5   Si, à la date d'expiration du certificat, le navire ne se trouve pas dans un port dans lequel il doit subir une visite, l'Administration peut proroger la validité de ce certificat. Toutefois, une telle prorogation ne doit être accordée que pour permettre au navire d'achever son voyage vers le port dans lequel il doit être visité et ce, uniquement dans le cas où cette mesure semble opportune et raisonnable. Aucun certificat ne doit être ainsi prorogé pour une période de plus de trois mois et un navire auquel cette prorogation a été accordée n'est pas en droit, en vertu de cette prorogation, après son arrivée dans le port dans lequel il doit être visité, d'en repartir sans avoir obtenu un nouveau certificat. Lorsque la visite de renouvellement est achevée, le nouveau certificat est valable pour une période n'excédant pas cinq ans à compter de la date d'expiration du certificat existant avant que la prorogation ait été accordée.

6 Un certificat délivré à un navire effectuant des voyages courts, qui n'a pas été prorogé conformément aux dispositions précédentes de la présente règle, peut être prorogé par l'Administration pour une période de grâce ne dépassant pas d'un mois la date d'expiration indiquée sur ce certificat. Lorsque la visite de renouvellement est achevée, le nouveau certificat est valable pour une période n'excédant pas cinq ans à compter de la date d'expiration du certificat existant avant que la prorogation ait été accordée.

7 Dans certains cas particuliers, tels qu'arrêtés par l'Administration, il n'est pas nécessaire que la validité du nouveau certificat commence à la date d'expiration du certificat existant conformément aux prescriptions du paragraphe 2.2, 5 ou 6 de la présente règle. Dans ces cas particuliers, le nouveau certificat est valable pour une période n'excédant pas cinq ans à compter de la date d'achèvement de la visite de renouvellement.

8 Lorsqu'une visite annuelle est effectuée dans un délai inférieur à celui qui est spécifié à la règle E-1 :

.1 la date anniversaire figurant sur le certificat est remplacée au moyen d'un visa par une date qui ne doit pas être postérieure de plus de trois mois à la date à laquelle la visite a été achevée;

.2 la visite annuelle ou intermédiaire suivante prescrite à la règle E-1 doit être achevée aux intervalles stipulés par cette règle, calculés à partir de la nouvelle date anniversaire;

.3 la date d'expiration peut demeurer inchangée à condition qu'une ou plusieurs visites annuelles, selon le cas, soient effectuées de telle sorte que les intervalles maximaux entre visites prescrits par la règle E-1 ne soient pas dépassés.

9 Un certificat délivré en vertu de la règle E-2 ou E-3 cesse d'être valable dans l'un quelconque des cas suivants :

.1 si la structure, l'équipement, les systèmes, les installations, les aménagements et les matériaux nécessaires pour satisfaire pleinement à la présente Convention ont fait l'objet d'un changement, d'un remplacement ou d'une réparation importante et si un visa n'a pas été apposé sur le certificat conformément à la présente Annexe;

.2 si un navire passe sous le pavillon d'un autre État. Un nouveau certificat ne doit être délivré que si la Partie délivrant le nouveau certificat a la certitude que le navire satisfait aux prescriptions de la règle E-1. Dans le cas d'un transfert de pavillon entre Parties, si la demande lui en est faite dans un délai de trois mois à compter du transfert, la Partie dont le navire était autorisé précédemment à battre le pavillon adresse dès que possible à l'Administration des copies du certificat dont le navire était muni avant le transfert, ainsi que des copies des rapports de visite, le cas échéant;

.3 si les visites pertinentes ne sont pas achevées dans les délais spécifiés à la règle E-1.1; ou

.4 si le visa prévu à la règle E-1.1 n'a pas été apposé sur le certificat.

Appendice I

Modèle de certificat international de gestion des eaux de ballast

CERTIFICAT INTERNATIONAL DE GESTION DES EAUX DE BALLAST

Délivré en vertu des dispositions de la Convention internationale pour le contrôle et la gestion des eaux de ballast et sédiments des navires (ci-après dénommée «la Convention») sous l'autorité du Gouvernement

. . . .

(Nom officiel complet du pays)

par . . . .

(Titre officiel complet de la personne compétente ou de l'organisme autorisé en vertu des dispositions de la Convention)

Caractéristiques du navire*

    Nom du navire . . . .

    Numéro ou lettres distinctifs . . . .

    Port d'immatriculation . . . .

    Jauge brute . . . .

    Numéro OMI† . . . .

    Date de construction . . . .

    Capacité en eaux de ballast (en mètres cubes) . . . .

Renseignements sur la(les) méthode(s) utilisée(s) pour procéder à la gestion des eaux de ballast

Méthode utilisée pour procéder à la gestion des eaux de ballast . . . .

    Date d'installation (s'il y a lieu) . . . .

    Nom du fabricant (s'il y a lieu) . . . .

---

* Les caractéristiques du navire peuvent aussi être présentées horizontalement dans des cases.
† Système de numéros OMI d'identification des navires que l'Organisation a adopté par la résolution A.600(15).

La(les) principale(s) méthode(s) utilisée(s) pour procéder à la gestion des eaux de ballast à bord du présent navire est(sont) :

□ conforme(s) à la règle D-1

□ conforme(s) à la règle D-2
(veuillez préciser) . . . .

□ le navire est soumis à la règle D-4

IL EST CERTIFIÉ :

1   que le navire a été visité conformément à la règle E-1 de l'Annexe de la Convention; et

2   qu'à la suite de cette visite, il a été constaté que la gestion des eaux de ballast à bord du navire satisfaisait aux dispositions de l'Annexe de la Convention.

Le présent certificat est valable jusqu'au . . . . sous réserve des visites prévues à la règle E-1 de l'Annexe de la Convention.

Date d'achèvement de la visite sur la base de laquelle le présent certificat est délivré : jour/mois/année

Délivré à . . . .
(Lieu de délivrance du certificat)

Le . . . .
(Date de délivrance)   *(Signature de l'agent autorisé qui délivre le certificat)*

(Cachet ou tampon, selon le cas, de l'autorité)

ATTESTATION DE VISITE(S) ANNUELLE(S) ET INTERMÉDIAIRE(S)

IL EST CERTIFIÉ que, lors d'une visite prescrite par la règle E-1 de l'Annexe de la Convention, il a été constaté que le navire satisfaisait aux dispositions pertinentes de la Convention.

Visite annuelle :   Signé . . . .
                                       (Signature de l'agent autorisé)

                                       Lieu . . . .

                                       Date . . . .

(Cachet ou tampon, selon le cas, de l'autorité)

Visite annuelle/intermédiaire* :   Signé . . . .
                                       (Signature de l'agent autorisé)

                                       Lieu . . . .

                                       Date . . . .

(Cachet ou tampon, selon le cas, de l'autorité)

Visite annuelle/intermédiaire* :   Signé . . . .
                                       (Signature de l'agent autorisé)

                                       Lieu . . . .

                                       Date . . . .

(Cachet ou tampon, selon le cas, de l'autorité)

Visite annuelle :   Signé . . . .
                                       (Signature de l'agent autorisé)

                                       Lieu . . . .

                                       Date . . . .

(Cachet ou tampon, selon le cas, de l'autorité)

---

* Rayer les mentions inutiles.

VISITE ANNUELLE/INTERMÉDIAIRE
EFFECTUÉE CONFORMÉMENT À LA RÈGLE E-5.8.3

IL EST CERTIFIÉ que, lors d'une visite annuelle/intermédiaire* effectuée conformément à la règle E-5.8.3 de l'Annexe de la Convention, il a été constaté que le navire satisfaisait aux dispositions pertinentes de la Convention.

Signé ....
(Signature de l'agent autorisé)

Lieu ....

Date ....

(Cachet ou tampon, selon le cas, de l'autorité)

VISA DE PROROGATION DU CERTIFICAT S'IL EST VALABLE POUR UNE DURÉE INFÉRIEURE À 5 ANS, EN CAS D'APPLICATION DE LA RÈGLE E-5.3

Le navire satisfait aux dispositions pertinentes de la Convention et le présent certificat, conformément à la règle E-5.3 de l'Annexe de la Convention, est accepté comme valable jusqu'au ....

Signé ....
(Signature de l'agent autorisé)

Lieu ....

Date ....

(Cachet ou tampon, selon le cas, de l'autorité)

VISA APPOSÉ APRÈS ACHÈVEMENT DE LA VISITE DE RENOUVELLEMENT, EN CAS D'APPLICATION DE LA RÈGLE E-5.4

Le navire satisfait aux dispositions pertinentes de la Convention et le présent certificat, conformément à la règle E-5.4 de l'Annexe de la Convention, est accepté comme valable jusqu'au ....

Signé ....
(Signature de l'agent autorisé)

Lieu ....

Date ....

(Cachet ou tampon, selon le cas, de l'autorité)

---

* Rayer les mentions inutiles.

VISA DE PROROGATION DE LA VALIDITÉ DU CERTIFICAT JUSQU'À CE QUE LE NAVIRE ARRIVE DANS LE PORT DE VISITE OU POUR UNE PÉRIODE DE GRÂCE, EN CAS D'APPLICATION DE LA RÈGLE E-5.5 OU E-5.6

Le présent certificat, conformément à la règle E-5.5 ou E-5.6* de l'Annexe de la Convention, est accepté comme valable jusqu'au . . . .

Signé . . . .
(Signature de l'agent autorisé)

Lieu . . . .

Date . . . .

(Cachet ou tampon, selon le cas, de l'autorité)

VISA POUR L'AVANCEMENT DE LA DATE ANNIVERSAIRE, EN CAS D'APPLICATION DE LA RÈGLE E-5.8

Conformément à la règle E-5.8 de l'Annexe de la Convention, la nouvelle date anniversaire est fixée au . . . .

Signé . . . .
(Signature de l'agent autorisé)

Lieu . . . .

Date . . . .

(Cachet ou tampon, selon le cas, de l'autorité)

Conformément à la règle E-5.8 de l'Annexe de la Convention, la nouvelle date anniversaire est fixée au . . . .

Signé . . . .
(Signature de l'agent autorisé)

Lieu . . . .

Date . . . .

(Cachet ou tampon, selon le cas, de l'autorité)

---

* Rayer les mentions inutiles.

81

Appendice II

Modèle de registre des eaux de ballast

CONVENTION INTERNATIONALE POUR LE CONTRÔLE ET LA GESTION
DES EAUX DE BALLAST ET SÉDIMENTS DES NAVIRES

Période allant du . . . . au . . . .

Nom du navire . . . .

Numéro OMI . . . .

Jauge brute . . . .

Pavillon . . . .

Capacité totale en eaux de ballast (en mètres cubes) . . . .

Le navire est muni d'un plan de gestion des eaux de ballast ☐

Schéma du navire indiquant les citernes à ballast :

1   Introduction

Conformément à la règle B-2 de l'Annexe de la Convention internationale pour le contrôle et la gestion des eaux de ballast et sédiments des navires, il doit être tenu un registre dans lequel est consignée chaque opération concernant les eaux de ballast, y compris les rejets effectués en mer et dans des installations de réception.

2   Eaux de ballast et gestion des eaux de ballast

L'expression «eaux de ballast» désigne les eaux et les matières en suspension chargées à bord d'un navire pour contrôler l'assiette, la gîte, le tirant d'eau, la stabilité ou les contraintes. La gestion des eaux de ballast doit être conforme à un plan approuvé de gestion des eaux de ballast et tenir compte des Directives[*] élaborées par l'Organisation.

---

[*] Il convient de se reporter aux Directives relatives au contrôle et à la gestion des eaux de ballast des navires en vue de réduire au minimum le transfert d'organismes aquatiques nuisibles et d'agents pathogènes que l'Organisation a adoptées par la résolution A.868(20).

3 Mentions portées sur le registre des eaux de ballast

Des mentions doivent être portées sur le registre des eaux de ballast à chacune des occasions suivantes :

3.1 Lorsque le navire prend de l'eau de ballast :

.1 Date, heure et lieu, port ou installation, de la prise de ballast (port ou latitude/longitude), profondeur si en dehors du port

.2 Estimation du volume de ballast pris à bord, en mètres cubes

.3 Signature de l'officier chargé de l'opération

3.2 Chaque fois que de l'eau de ballast est mise en circulation ou traitée aux fins de la gestion des eaux de ballast :

.1 Date et heure de l'opération

.2 Estimation du volume mis en circulation ou traité (en mètres cubes)

.3 L'opération a-t-elle été menée conformément au plan de gestion des eaux de ballast ?

.4 Signature de l'officier chargé de l'opération

3.3 Lorsque l'eau de ballast est rejetée à la mer :

.1 Date, heure et lieu, port ou installation, du rejet (port ou latitude/longitude)

.2 Estimation du volume de ballast rejeté, en mètres cubes, et du volume restant, en mètres cubes

.3 Le plan approuvé de gestion des eaux de ballast a-t-il été mis en oeuvre avant le rejet ?

.4 Signature de l'officier chargé de l'opération

3.4 Lorsque de l'eau de ballast est rejetée dans une installation de réception :

.1 Date, heure et lieu de la prise de ballast

.2 Date, heure et lieu du rejet de ballast

.3 Port ou installation

.4 Estimation du volume de ballast rejeté ou pris en mètres cubes

.5 Le plan approuvé de gestion des eaux de ballast a-t-il été mis en oeuvre avant le rejet ?

.6 Signature de l'officier chargé de l'opération

3.5 Rejet accidentel ou autre prise ou rejet exceptionnel d'eau de ballast

.1 Date et heure à laquelle le rejet ou la prise de ballast s'est produit

.2 Port ou position du navire au moment du rejet ou de la prise de ballast

.3 Estimation du volume de ballast rejeté

.4 Circonstances de la prise, du rejet, de la fuite ou de la perte de ballast, cause et observations générales

.5 Le plan approuvé de gestion des eaux de ballast a-t-il été mis en oeuvre avant le rejet ?

.6 Signature de l'officier chargé de l'opération

3.6 Procédures d'exploitation supplémentaires et observations générales

4   Volume d'eau de ballast

Le volume d'eau de ballast à bord du navire devrait être estimé en mètres cubes. Le registre des eaux de ballast se réfère à maintes reprises à l'estimation du volume d'eau de ballast. Il est reconnu que la précision avec laquelle les volumes sont estimés est sujette à interprétation.

REGISTRE DES OPÉRATIONS CONCERNANT LES EAUX DE BALLAST

EXEMPLE DE PAGE DU REGISTRE DES EAUX DE BALLAST

Nom du navire . . . .

Numéro ou lettres distinctifs . . . .

Date	Rubrique (numéro)	Opération/signature de l'officier responsable

Signature du capitaine . . . .

DOCUMENT JOINT

RÉSOLUTIONS ADOPTÉES PAR LA CONFÉRENCE

Résolution 1

Travaux futurs de l'Organisation concernant la Convention internationale pour le contrôle et la gestion des eaux de ballast et sédiments des navires

LA CONFÉRENCE,

AYANT ADOPTÉ la Convention internationale pour le contrôle et la gestion des eaux de ballast et sédiments des navires (ci-après dénommée «la Convention»),

NOTANT que les articles 5 et 9 et les règles A-4, A-5, B-1, B-3, B-4, B-5, C-1, D-3 et D-4 de l'Annexe de la Convention renvoient aux directives ou procédures qui doivent être élaborées par l'Organisation et qui doivent porter sur des questions spécifiques indiquées dans ces articles et règles,

RECONNAISSANT qu'il est nécessaire d'élaborer les directives en question afin de garantir l'application uniforme à l'échelle mondiale des prescriptions pertinentes de la Convention,

INVITE l'Organisation à élaborer de toute urgence :

.1 des directives pour les installations de réception des sédiments en vertu de l'article 5 et de la règle B-5;

.2 des directives pour l'échantillonnage des eaux de ballast en vertu de l'article 9;

.3 des directives sur le respect de conditions équivalentes pour la gestion des eaux de ballast à l'intention des bateaux de plaisance et des engins de recherche et de sauvetage en vertu de la règle A-5;

.4 des directives sur le plan de gestion des eaux de ballast en vertu de la règle B-1;

.5 des directives pour les installations de réception des eaux de ballast en vertu de la règle B-3;

.6 des directives pour le renouvellement des eaux de ballast en vertu de la règle B-4;

.7 des directives concernant les mesures supplémentaires prises en vertu de la règle C-1 et l'évaluation des risques en vertu de la règle A-4;

.8   des directives pour l'approbation des systèmes de gestion des eaux de ballast en vertu de la règle D-3.1;

.9   procédure d'approbation des substances actives en vertu de la règle D-3.2; et

.10 des directives concernant les prototypes de technologies de traitement des eaux de ballast en vertu de la règle D-4,

et à les adopter le plus tôt possible et, en tout cas, avant l'entrée en vigueur de la Convention afin de faciliter l'application uniforme à l'échelle mondiale de la présente Convention.

Résolution 2

Utilisation d'outils décisionnels pour l'examen des normes en application de la règle D-5

LA CONFÉRENCE,

AYANT ADOPTÉ la Convention internationale pour le contrôle et la gestion des eaux de ballast et sédiments des navires (ci-après dénommée «la Convention»),

NOTANT que la règle D-5 de la Convention exige que lors d'une réunion qu'il tiendra au plus tard trois ans avant la date la plus proche à laquelle la norme de la règle D-2 prendra effet, le Comité entreprenne un examen visant à déterminer s'il existe des technologies permettant de satisfaire à ladite norme, à évaluer les critères énoncés au paragraphe 2 de la règle D-5 et à analyser les effets socio-économiques eu égard, en particulier, aux besoins des pays en développement et notamment des petits États insulaires en développement,

RECONNAISSANT que des outils décisionnels sont utiles pour procéder à des évaluations complexes,

RECOMMANDE que l'Organisation utilise des outils décisionnels appropriés pour procéder à l'examen des normes conformément à la règle D-5 de la Convention; et

INVITE les États Membres à fournir des avis à l'Organisation sur les outils décisionnels utiles et fiables qui pourraient l'aider à procéder à cet examen.

Résolution 3
Promotion de la coopération et de l'assistance techniques

LA CONFÉRENCE,

AYANT ADOPTÉ la Convention internationale pour le contrôle et la gestion des eaux de ballast et sédiments des navires (ci-après dénommée «la Convention»),

CONSCIENTE du fait que les Parties à la Convention seront appelées à donner pleinement et entièrement effet à ses dispositions de manière à prévenir, réduire au minimum et finalement, éliminer le transfert d'organismes aquatiques nuisibles et d'agents pathogènes au moyen du contrôle et de la gestion des eaux de ballast et sédiments des navires,

NOTANT qu'en vertu des articles 13.1 et 13.2 de la Convention, les Parties sont tenues notamment de fournir un appui aux Parties qui demandent une assistance technique pour le contrôle et la gestion des eaux de ballast et sédiments des navires,

RECONNAISSANT la valeur des activités de coopération technique menées dans le cadre d'un partenariat avec les pays en développement sur les questions relatives à la gestion des eaux de ballast en vertu du Programme mondial FEM/PNUD/OMI sur la gestion des eaux de ballast (Programme GloBallast) depuis 2000,

CONVAINCUE que la promotion de la coopération technique permettra d'accélérer l'acceptation, l'interprétation uniforme et l'application de la Convention par les États,

NOTANT AVEC SATISFACTION que, par l'adoption de la résolution A.901(21), l'Assemblée de l'Organisation maritime internationale (OMI) :

a) a affirmé que les travaux de l'OMI visant à élaborer des normes maritimes mondiales et à fournir une coopération technique en vue de garantir leur mise en oeuvre et leur application efficaces peuvent contribuer et contribuent véritablement au développement durable; et

b) a décidé que la mission de l'OMI, en ce qui concerne la coopération technique dans les années 2000, doit être d'aider les pays en développement à renforcer leur capacité à satisfaire aux règles et normes internationales relatives à la sécurité maritime ainsi qu'à la prévention de la pollution des mers et à la lutte contre celle-ci, en donnant la priorité aux programmes d'assistance technique axés sur la mise en valeur des ressources humaines, en particulier par le biais de la formation, et le renforcement des capacités institutionnelles,

1.   PRIE les États Membres, en coopération avec l'OMI, d'autres États et organismes internationaux intéressés, les organisations internationales ou régionales compétentes et les programmes de l'industrie, d'encourager et de fournir directement, ou par l'intermédiaire de l'OMI, un appui aux États qui sollicitent une assistance technique pour :

   a)   évaluer les incidences de la ratification, l'acceptation, l'approbation de la Convention ou de l'adhésion à celle-ci, ainsi que de sa mise en oeuvre et de son application;

   b)   mettre au point la législation nationale et les modalités institutionnelles pour donner effet à la Convention;

   c)   former le personnel scientifique et technique à la recherche, la surveillance et la mise en application (par exemple, évaluation des risques liés aux eaux de ballast, études sur les espèces marines envahissantes, surveillance et systèmes d'alerte rapide, échantillonnage et analyse des eaux de ballast), y compris, le cas échéant, fournir le matériel et les installations nécessaires en vue de renforcer les capacités nationales;

   d)   échanger des renseignements et des services de coopération technique en vue de réduire au minimum les risques pour l'environnement et la santé humaine dus au transfert d'organismes aquatiques nuisibles et d'agents pathogènes, au moyen du contrôle et de la gestion des eaux de ballast et sédiments des navires;

   e)   encourager la recherche-développement sur les méthodes améliorées de gestion et de traitement des eaux de ballast; et

   f)   établir des prescriptions spéciales dans certaines zones conformément à la section C des règles de la Convention;

2.   PRIE EN OUTRE les agences et organismes internationaux d'aide au développement d'apporter leur appui, notamment en fournissant les ressources nécessaires, aux programmes de coopération technique dans le domaine du contrôle et de la gestion des eaux de ballast d'une manière qui soit compatible avec les dispositions de la Convention;

3.   INVITE le Comité de la coopération technique de l'OMI à continuer à prévoir des activités pour le renforcement des capacités en matière de contrôle et de gestion des eaux de ballast et sédiments des navires, dans le cadre du Programme intégré de coopération technique de l'Organisation, afin d'appuyer la mise en oeuvre et l'application effectives de la Convention par les pays en développement; et

4.   PRIE INSTAMMENT tous les États d'entreprendre une action répondant aux mesures de coopération technique susmentionnées sans attendre l'entrée en vigueur de la Convention.

Résolution 4

Examen de l'annexe de la Convention internationale pour le contrôle et la gestion des eaux de ballast et sédiments des navires

LA CONFÉRENCE,

AYANT ADOPTÉ la Convention internationale pour le contrôle et la gestion des eaux de ballast et sédiments des navires (la Convention),

RECONNAISSANT qu'il faudra peut-être envisager de revoir l'Annexe de la Convention et en particulier, sans toutefois s'y limiter, les règles A-4, A-5, B-1, B-3, B-4, C-1, D-1, D-2, D-3 et D-5, avant l'entrée en vigueur de la Convention, par exemple si des obstacles semblent entraver cette entrée en vigueur ou afin de passer en revue les normes décrites dans la règle D-2 de l'Annexe de la Convention,

RECOMMANDE que le Comité de la protection du milieu marin examine les règles de l'Annexe de la Convention lorsqu'il le jugera nécessaire, mais au plus tard trois ans avant la date la plus proche à laquelle les normes décrites dans la règle D-2 de l'Annexe de la Convention prendront effet, à savoir 2006.

CONVENIO INTERNACIONAL PARA EL CONTROL Y LA GESTIÓN DEL AGUA DE LASTRE Y LOS SEDIMENTOS DE LOS BUQUES, 2004

LAS PARTES EN EL PRESENTE CONVENIO,

RECORDANDO el artículo 196 1) de la Convención de las Naciones Unidas sobre el Derecho del Mar, 1982 (CONVEMAR), que estipula que "los Estados tomarán todas las medidas necesarias para prevenir, reducir y controlar la contaminación del medio marino causada por la utilización de tecnologías bajo su jurisdicción o control, o la introducción intencional o accidental en un sector determinado del medio marino de especies extrañas o nuevas que puedan causar en él cambios considerables y perjudiciales",

TOMANDO NOTA de los objetivos del Convenio sobre la Diversidad Biológica de 1992 y de que la transferencia e introducción de organismos acuáticos perjudiciales y agentes patógenos por conducto del agua de lastre de los buques suponen una amenaza para la conservación y la utilización sostenible de la diversidad biológica, así como de la decisión IV/5 de la Conferencia de las Partes en el Convenio sobre la Diversidad Biológica de 1998 (COP 4), relativa a la conservación y utilización sostenible de los ecosistemas marinos y costeros, y de la decisión VI/23 de la Conferencia de las Partes en el Convenio sobre la Diversidad Biológica de 2002 (COP 6), sobre las especies exóticas que amenazan los ecosistemas, los hábitats o las especies, incluidos los principios de orientación sobre especies invasoras,

TOMANDO NOTA ASIMISMO de que la Conferencia de las Naciones Unidas sobre el Medio Ambiente y el Desarrollo de 1992 (CNUMAD) solicitó a la Organización Marítima Internacional (la Organización) que considerase la adopción de reglas apropiadas sobre la descarga del agua de lastre,

TENIENDO PRESENTE el planteamiento preventivo descrito en el principio 15 de la Declaración de Río sobre el Medio Ambiente y el Desarrollo, y al que se hace referencia en la resolución MEPC.67(37), aprobada por el Comité de Protección del Medio Marino de la Organización el 15 de septiembre de 1995,

TENIENDO TAMBIÉN PRESENTE que la Cumbre Mundial sobre el Desarrollo Sostenible de 2002, en el párrafo 34 b) de su Plan de aplicación, insta a que en todos los niveles se acelere la elaboración de medidas para hacer frente al problema de las especies foráneas invasoras de las aguas de lastre,

CONSCIENTES de que la descarga no controlada del agua de lastre y los sedimentos desde los buques ha ocasionado la transferencia de organismos acuáticos perjudiciales y agentes patógenos que han causado daños al medio ambiente, la salud de los seres humanos, los bienes y los recursos,

RECONOCIENDO la importancia que la Organización concede a esta cuestión, puesta de manifiesto por las resoluciones de la Asamblea

A.774(18), de 1993, y A.868(20), de 1997, adoptadas con el fin de tratar la transferencia de organismos acuáticos perjudiciales y agentes patógenos,

RECONOCIENDO ASIMISMO que varios Estados han adoptado medidas individuales con miras a prevenir, reducir al mínimo y, en último término, eliminar los riesgos de introducción de organismos acuáticos perjudiciales y agentes patógenos por los buques que entran en sus puertos, y que esta cuestión, al ser de interés mundial, exige medidas basadas en reglas aplicables a escala mundial, junto con directrices para su implantación efectiva y su interpretación uniforme,

DESEANDO seguir con la elaboración de opciones más seguras y eficaces para la gestión del agua de lastre, que redunden en la prevención, la reducción al mínimo y, en último término, la eliminación sostenida de la transferencia de organismos acuáticos perjudiciales y agentes patógenos,

DECIDIDAS a prevenir, reducir al mínimo y, en último término, eliminar los riesgos para el medio ambiente, la salud de los seres humanos, los bienes y los recursos resultantes de la transferencia de organismos acuáticos perjudiciales y agentes patógenos por medio del control y la gestión del agua de lastre y los sedimentos de los buques, así como a evitar los efectos secundarios ocasionados por dicho control y promover los avances de los conocimientos y la tecnología conexos,

CONSIDERANDO que tales objetivos pueden cumplirse más eficazmente mediante un convenio internacional para el control y la gestión del agua de lastre y los sedimentos de los buques,

HAN CONVENIDO lo siguiente:

Artículo 1
Definiciones

Salvo indicación expresa en otro sentido, a los efectos del presente Convenio regirán las siguientes definiciones:

1   *Administración*: el Gobierno del Estado bajo cuya autoridad opere el buque. Respecto de un buque con derecho a enarbolar el pabellón de un Estado, la Administración es el Gobierno de ese Estado. Respecto de las plataformas flotantes dedicadas a la exploración y explotación del lecho marino y su subsuelo adyacente a la costa sobre la que el Estado ribereño ejerza derechos soberanos a efectos de exploración y explotación de sus recursos naturales, incluidas las unidades flotantes de almacenamiento (UFA) y las unidades flotantes de producción, almacenamiento y descarga (unidades FPAD), la Administración es el Gobierno del Estado ribereño en cuestión.

2   *Agua de lastre*: el agua, con las materias en suspensión que contenga, cargada a bordo de un buque para controlar el asiento, la escora, el calado, la estabilidad y los esfuerzos del buque.

3   *Gestión del agua de lastre*: procedimientos mecánicos, físicos, químicos o biológicos, ya sean utilizados individualmente o en combinación, destinados a extraer o neutralizar los organismos acuáticos perjudiciales y agentes patógenos existentes en el agua de lastre y los sedimentos, o a evitar la toma o la descarga de los mismos.

4 *Certificado*: el Certificado internacional de gestión del agua de lastre.

5 *Comité*: el Comité de Protección del Medio Marino de la Organización.

6 *Convenio*: el Convenio internacional para el control y la gestión del agua de lastre y los sedimentos de los buques.

7 *Arqueo bruto*: el arqueo bruto calculado de acuerdo con las reglas para la determinación del arqueo recogidas en el Anexo I del Convenio internacional sobre arqueo de buques, 1969, o en cualquier convenio que suceda a éste.

8 *Organismos acuáticos perjudiciales y agentes patógenos*: los organismos acuáticos y agentes patógenos cuya introducción en el mar, incluidos los estuarios, o en cursos de agua dulce pueda ocasionar riesgos para el medio ambiente, la salud de los seres humanos, los bienes o los recursos, deteriorar la diversidad biológica o entorpecer otros usos legítimos de tales zonas.

9 *Organización*: la Organización Marítima Internacional.

10 *Secretario General*: el Secretario General de la Organización.

11 *Sedimentos*: las materias que se depositen en el buque procedentes del agua de lastre.

12 *Buque*: toda nave, del tipo que sea, que opere en el medio acuático, incluidos los sumergibles, los artefactos flotantes, las plataformas flotantes, las UFA y las unidades FPAD.

Artículo 2
Obligaciones de carácter general

1 Las Partes se comprometen a hacer plena y totalmente efectivas las disposiciones del presente Convenio y de su anexo con objeto de prevenir, reducir al mínimo y, en último término, eliminar la transferencia de organismos acuáticos perjudiciales y agentes patógenos mediante el control y la gestión del agua de lastre y los sedimentos de los buques.

2 El anexo forma parte integrante del presente Convenio. Salvo indicación expresa en otro sentido, toda referencia al presente Convenio constituye también una referencia al anexo.

3 Nada de lo dispuesto en el presente Convenio se interpretará en el sentido de que se impide a una Parte adoptar, individualmente o junto con otras Partes, y de conformidad con el derecho internacional, medidas más rigurosas para la prevención, reducción o eliminación de la transferencia de organismos acuáticos perjudiciales y agentes patógenos mediante el control y la gestión del agua de lastre y los sedimentos de los buques.

4   Las Partes se esforzarán por colaborar en la implantación, aplicación y cumplimiento efectivos del presente Convenio.

5   Las Partes se comprometen a fomentar el desarrollo continuo de la gestión del agua de lastre y de normas para prevenir, reducir al mínimo y, en ultimo término, eliminar la transferencia de organismos acuáticos perjudiciales y agentes patógenos mediante el control y la gestión del agua de lastre y los sedimentos de los buques.

6   Las Partes que adopten medidas de conformidad con el presente Convenio se esforzarán por no dañar ni deteriorar el medio ambiente, la salud de los seres humanos, los bienes o los recursos, propios o de otros Estados.

7   Las Partes deberían garantizar que las prácticas de gestión del agua de lastre observadas para cumplir el presente Convenio no causan mayores daños al medio ambiente, la salud de los seres humanos, los bienes o los recursos, propios o de otros Estados, que los que previenen.

8   Las Partes alentarán a los buques que tengan derecho a enarbolar su pabellón y a los que se aplique el presente Convenio a que eviten, en la medida de lo posible, la toma de agua de lastre que pueda contener organismos acuáticos perjudiciales y agentes patógenos, así como los sedimentos que puedan contener dichos organismos, y para ello fomentarán la implantación adecuada de las recomendaciones elaboradas por la Organización.

9   Las Partes se esforzarán para cooperar bajo los auspicios de la Organización a fin de hacer frente a las amenazas y riesgos para la biodiversidad y los ecosistemas marinos sensibles, vulnerables o amenazados en las zonas situadas fuera de los límites de la jurisdicción nacional respecto de la gestión del agua de lastre.

Artículo 3
Ámbito de aplicación

1   Salvo indicación expresa en otro sentido, el presente Convenio se aplicará a:

a) los buques que tengan derecho a enarbolar el pabellón de una Parte; y

b) los buques que, sin tener derecho a enarbolar el pabellón de una Parte, operen bajo la autoridad de una Parte.

2   El presente Convenio no se aplicará a:

a) los buques que no estén proyectados o construidos para llevar agua de lastre;

b) los buques de una Parte que operen únicamente en aguas bajo la jurisdicción de esa Parte, salvo que ésta determine que la descarga del agua de lastre de los buques dañaría o deterioraría el medio ambiente, la salud de los seres humanos, los bienes o los recursos, propios, de los Estados adyacentes o de otros Estados;

c) los buques de una Parte que operen únicamente en aguas bajo la jurisdicción de otra Parte, a reserva de que esta Parte autorice la exclusión. Ninguna Parte concederá tal autorización si, en virtud de la misma, se daña o deteriora el medio ambiente, la salud de los seres humanos, los bienes o los recursos, propios, de los Estados adyacentes o de otros Estados. Toda Parte que no conceda tal autorización notificará a la Administración del buque en cuestión que el presente Convenio se aplica a ese buque;

d) los buques que operen únicamente en aguas situadas bajo la jurisdicción de una Parte y en alta mar, a excepción de los buques a los que no se haya concedido una autorización de conformidad con lo indicado en el apartado c), salvo que dicha Parte determine que la descarga del agua de lastre de los buques dañaría o deterioraría el medio ambiente, la salud de los seres humanos, los bienes o los recursos, propios, de los Estados adyacentes o de otros Estados;

e) los buques de guerra, ni a los buques auxiliares de la armada, ni a los buques que, siendo propiedad de un Estado o estando explotados por él, estén exclusivamente dedicados en el momento de que se trate a servicios gubernamentales de carácter no comercial. No obstante, cada Parte garantizará, mediante la adopción de medidas apropiadas que no menoscaben las operaciones o la capacidad operativa de tales buques, que éstos operen, dentro de lo razonable y factible, de forma compatible con lo prescrito en el presente Convenio; y

f) el agua de lastre permanente en tanques precintados que no se descarga.

3   Por lo que respecta a los buques de Estados que no sean Partes en el presente Convenio, las Partes aplicarán las prescripciones del presente Convenio según sea necesario para garantizar que no se dé un trato más favorable a tales buques.

Artículo 4
Control de la transferencia de organismos acuáticos
perjudiciales y agentes patógenos por el agua de lastre
y los sedimentos de los buques

1   Cada Parte prescribirá que los buques a los que sean aplicables las disposiciones del presente Convenio y que tengan derecho a enarbolar su pabellón o que operen bajo su autoridad cumplan las prescripciones del presente Convenio, incluidas las normas y prescripciones aplicables del anexo, y adoptará medidas efectivas para garantizar que tales buques cumplan dichas prescripciones.

2   Cada Parte elaborará, teniendo debidamente en cuenta sus propias condiciones y capacidades, políticas, estrategias o programas nacionales para la gestión del agua de lastre en sus puertos y en las aguas bajo su jurisdicción que sean acordes con los objetivos del presente Convenio y contribuyan a lograrlos.

Artículo 5
Instalaciones de recepción de sedimentos

1   Cada Parte se compromete a garantizar que en los puertos y terminales designados por ella en los que se efectúen trabajos de reparación o de limpieza de tanques de lastre se disponga de instalaciones adecuadas para la recepción de sedimentos, teniendo en cuenta las directrices elaboradas por la Organización. Tales instalaciones de recepción funcionarán de forma que no ocasionen demoras innecesarias a los buques que las utilicen y dispondrán de los medios necesarios para la eliminación segura de tales sedimentos sin deteriorar ni dañar el medio ambiente, la salud de los seres humanos, los bienes o los recursos, propios o de otros Estados.

2   Cada Parte notificará a la Organización, para que ésta lo comunique a las demás Partes interesadas, todos los casos en que las instalaciones establecidas en virtud de lo dispuesto en el párrafo 1 sean presuntamente inadecuadas.

Artículo 6
Investigación científica y técnica y labor de vigilancia

1   Las Partes se esforzarán, individual o conjuntamente, por:

a)   fomentar y facilitar la investigación científica y técnica sobre la gestión del agua de lastre; y

b)   vigilar los efectos de la gestión del agua de lastre en las aguas bajo su jurisdicción.

Dicha labor de investigación y vigilancia debería incluir la observación, la medición, el muestreo, la evaluación y el análisis de la eficacia y las repercusiones negativas de cualquier tecnología o metodología empleadas, así como de cualesquiera repercusiones negativas debidas a los organismos y agentes patógenos cuya transferencia por el agua de lastre de los buques se haya determinado.

2   A fin de promover los objetivos del presente Convenio, cada Parte facilitará a las demás Partes que lo soliciten la información pertinente sobre:

a)   los programas científicos y tecnológicos y las medidas de carácter técnico acometidas con respecto a la gestión del agua de lastre; y

b)   la eficacia de la gestión del agua de lastre deducida de los programas de evaluación y vigilancia.

Artículo 7
Reconocimiento y certificación

1   Cada Parte se cerciorará de que los buques que enarbolen su pabellón o que operen bajo su autoridad, y que estén sujetos a reconocimiento y certificación, se reconocen y certifican de conformidad con las reglas del anexo.

2   Toda Parte que implante medidas en virtud del artículo 2.3 y de la sección C del anexo no exigirá ningún reconocimiento ni certificación adicional a un buque de otra Parte, y la Administración del buque no estará obligada a efectuar ningún reconocimiento ni certificación respecto de las medidas adicionales impuestas por otra Parte. La verificación de tales medidas adicionales será responsabilidad de la Parte que las implante y no ocasionará demoras innecesarias al buque.

Artículo 8
Infracciones

1 Toda infracción de las disposiciones del presente Convenio estará penada con las sanciones que a tal efecto establecerá la legislación de la Administración del buque de que se trate, independientemente de donde ocurra la infracción. Cuando se notifique una infracción a una Administración, ésta investigará el asunto y podrá pedir a la Parte notificante que proporcione pruebas adicionales de la presunta infracción. Si la Administración estima que hay pruebas suficientes para incoar proceso respecto de la presunta infracción, hará que se incoe lo antes posible de conformidad con su legislación. La Administración comunicará inmediatamente a la Parte que le haya notificado la presunta infracción, así como a la Organización, las medidas que adopte. Si la Administración no ha tomado ninguna medida en el plazo de un año, informará al respecto a la Parte que le haya notificado la presunta infracción.

2 Toda infracción de las disposiciones del presente Convenio que se cometa dentro de la jurisdicción de una Parte estará penada con las sanciones que establecerá la legislación de esa Parte. Siempre que se cometa una infracción así, la Parte interesada:

a) hará que se incoe proceso de conformidad con su legislación; o bien

b) facilitará a la Administración del buque de que se trate toda la información y las pruebas que obren en su poder con respecto a la infracción cometida.

3 Las sanciones previstas por la legislación de una Parte conforme a lo dispuesto en el presente artículo serán suficientemente severas para disuadir a los eventuales infractores del presente Convenio, dondequiera que se encuentren.

Artículo 9
Inspección de buques

1 Todo buque al que sean aplicables las disposiciones del presente Convenio podrá ser objeto, en cualquier puerto o terminal mar adentro de otra Parte, de una inspección por funcionarios debidamente autorizados por dicha Parte a los efectos de determinar si el buque cumple las disposiciones del presente Convenio. Salvo por lo dispuesto en el párrafo 2 del presente artículo, dichas inspecciones se limitarán a:

a) verificar que existe a bordo un Certificado válido, el cual será aceptado si se considera válido; y

b) inspeccionar el Libro registro del agua de lastre; y/o

c) realizar un muestreo del agua de lastre del buque de conformidad con las directrices que elabore la Organización. No obstante, el tiempo necesario para analizar las muestras no se utilizará como fundamento para retrasar innecesariamente las operaciones, el movimiento o la salida del buque.

2 Si el buque no lleva un Certificado válido o si existen motivos fundados para pensar que:

a) el estado del buque o del equipo no se corresponden en lo esencial con los pormenores del Certificado; o

b) el capitán o la tripulación no están familiarizados con los procedimientos fundamentales de a bordo en relación con la gestión del agua de lastre, o no han implantado tales procedimientos,

podrá efectuarse una inspección pormenorizada.

3 Cuando se den las circunstancias indicadas en el párrafo 2 del presente artículo, la Parte que efectúe la inspección tomará las medidas necesarias para garantizar que el buque no descargará agua de lastre hasta que pueda hacerlo sin presentar un riesgo para el medio ambiente, la salud de los seres humanos, los bienes o los recursos.

Artículo 10
Detección de infracciones y control de buques

1 Las Partes cooperarán en la detección de infracciones y en el cumplimiento de las disposiciones del presente Convenio.

2 Si se detecta que un buque ha infringido el presente Convenio, la Parte cuyo pabellón el buque tenga derecho a enarbolar, y/o la Parte en cuyo puerto o terminal mar adentro esté operando el buque, podrá adoptar, además de cualquier sanción descrita en el artículo 8 o cualquier medida descrita en el artículo 9, medidas para amonestar, detener o excluir al buque. No obstante, la Parte en cuyo puerto o terminal mar adentro esté operando el buque podrá conceder al buque permiso para salir del puerto o terminal mar adentro con el fin de descargar agua de lastre o de dirigirse al astillero de reparaciones o la instalación de recepción más próximos disponibles, a condición de que ello no represente un riesgo para el medio ambiente, la salud de los seres humanos, los bienes o los recursos.

3 Si el muestreo descrito en el artículo 9.1 c) arroja unos resultados, o respalda la información recibida de otro puerto o terminal mar adentro, que indiquen que el buque representa un riesgo para el medio ambiente, la salud de los seres humanos, los bienes o los recursos, la Parte en cuyas aguas esté operando el buque prohibirá a dicho buque que descargue agua de lastre hasta que se elimine tal riesgo.

4 Una Parte también podrá inspeccionar un buque que entre en un puerto o terminal mar adentro bajo su jurisdicción si cualquier otra Parte presenta una solicitud de investigación, junto con pruebas suficientes de que el buque infringe o ha infringido lo dispuesto en el presente Convenio. El informe de dicha investigación se enviará a la Parte que la haya solicitado y a la autoridad competente de la Administración del buque en cuestión para que puedan adoptarse las medidas oportunas.

Artículo 11
Notificación de las medidas de control

1   Si una inspección efectuada en virtud de los artículos 9 ó 10 indica una infracción del presente Convenio, se informará de ello al buque, y se remitirá un informe a la Administración, incluida cualquier prueba de la infracción.

2   En caso de que se tomen medidas en virtud de los artículos 9.3, 10.2 ó 10.3, el funcionario que aplique tales medidas informará inmediatamente, por escrito, a la Administración del buque en cuestión o, si esto no es posible, al cónsul o representante diplomático del buque de que se trate, dando cuenta de todas las circunstancias por las cuales se estimó necesario adoptar medidas. Además, se informará a la organización reconocida responsable de la expedición de los certificados.

3   La autoridad del Estado rector del puerto de que se trate facilitará toda la información pertinente sobre la infracción al siguiente puerto de escala, además de a las partes a que se hace referencia en el párrafo 2, si no puede tomar las medidas especificadas en los artículos 9.3, 10.2 ó 10.3 o si ha autorizado al buque a dirigirse al próximo puerto de escala.

Artículo 12
Demoras innecesarias causadas a los buques

1   Se hará todo lo posible para evitar que un buque sufra una detención o demora innecesaria a causa de las medidas que se adopten de conformidad con los artículos 7.2, 8, 9 ó 10.

2   Cuando un buque haya sufrido una detención o demora innecesaria a causa de las medidas adoptadas de conformidad con los artículos 7.2, 8, 9 ó 10, dicho buque tendrá derecho a una indemnización por todo daño o perjuicio que haya sufrido.

Artículo 13
Asistencia técnica, cooperación
y cooperación regional

1   Las Partes se comprometen, directamente o a través de la Organización y otros organismos internacionales, según proceda, en lo que respecta al control y la gestión del agua de lastre y los sedimentos de los buques, a facilitar a las Partes que soliciten asistencia técnica apoyo destinado a:

   a)   formar personal;

   b)   garantizar la disponibilidad de tecnologías, equipo e instalaciones pertinentes;

   c)   iniciar programas conjuntos de investigación y desarrollo; y

d) emprender otras medidas tendentes a la implantación efectiva del presente Convenio y de las orientaciones relativas a éste elaboradas por la Organización.

2 Las Partes se comprometen a cooperar activamente, con arreglo a sus legislaciones, reglamentos y políticas nacionales, en la transferencia de tecnología relacionada con el control y la gestión del agua de lastre y los sedimentos de los buques.

3 Para la promoción de los objetivos del presente Convenio, las Partes con intereses comunes en la protección del medio ambiente, la salud de los seres humanos, los bienes y los recursos en una zona geográfica determinada, y en especial las Partes que limiten con mares cerrados o semicerrados, procurarán, teniendo presentes las características regionales distintivas, ampliar la cooperación regional, también mediante la celebración de acuerdos regionales en consonancia con el presente Convenio. Las Partes tratarán de colaborar con las partes en acuerdos regionales para la elaboración de procedimientos armonizados.

Artículo 14
Comunicación de información

1 Cada Parte comunicará a la Organización y, cuando proceda, pondrá a disposición de las demás Partes la siguiente información:

a) toda prescripción y procedimiento relativos a la gestión del agua de lastre, incluidas las leyes, reglamentos y directrices para la implantación del presente Convenio;

b) la existencia y ubicación de toda instalación de recepción para la eliminación del agua de lastre y los sedimentos sin riesgos para el medio ambiente; y

c) toda petición de información a un buque que no pueda cumplir las disposiciones del presente Convenio por las razones que se especifican en las reglas A-3 y B-4 del anexo.

2 La Organización notificará a las Partes toda comunicación que reciba en virtud del presente artículo y distribuirá a todas las Partes la información que le sea comunicada en virtud de lo dispuesto en los apartados 1 b) y 1 c) del presente artículo.

Artículo 15
Solución de controversias

Las Partes resolverán toda controversia que surja entre ellas respecto de la interpretación o aplicación del presente Convenio mediante negociación, investigación, mediación, conciliación, arbitraje, arreglo judicial, recurso a organismos o acuerdos regionales, o cualquier otro medio pacífico de su elección.

Artículo 16
*Relación con el derecho internacional
y con otros acuerdos*

Nada de lo dispuesto en el presente Convenio irá en perjuicio de los derechos y obligaciones de un Estado en virtud del derecho internacional consuetudinario recogido en la Convención de las Naciones Unidas sobre el Derecho del Mar.

Artículo 17
*Firma, ratificación, aceptación,
aprobación y adhesión*

1   El presente Convenio estará abierto a la firma de cualquier Estado en la sede de la Organización desde el 1 de junio de 2004 hasta el 31 de mayo de 2005 y después de ese plazo seguirá abierto a la adhesión de cualquier Estado.

2   Los Estados podrán constituirse en Partes en el presente Convenio mediante:

   a)   firma sin reserva en cuanto a ratificación, aceptación o aprobación; o

   b)   firma a reserva de ratificación, aceptación o aprobación, seguida de ratificación, aceptación o aprobación; o

   c)   adhesión.

3   La ratificación, aceptación, aprobación o adhesión se efectuarán depositando el instrumento correspondiente ante el Secretario General.

4   Todo Estado integrado por dos o más unidades territoriales en las que sea aplicable un régimen jurídico distinto en relación con las cuestiones que son objeto del presente Convenio podrá declarar en el momento de la firma, ratificación, aceptación, aprobación o adhesión que el presente Convenio será aplicable a todas sus unidades territoriales, o sólo a una o varias de ellas, y podrá en cualquier momento sustituir por otra su declaración original.

5   Esa declaración se notificará por escrito al depositario y en ella se hará constar expresamente a qué unidad o unidades territoriales será aplicable el presente Convenio.

Artículo 18
Entrada en vigor

1   El presente Convenio entrará en vigor doce meses después de la fecha en que por lo menos treinta Estados cuyas flotas mercantes combinadas representen no menos del treinta y cinco por ciento del tonelaje bruto de la marina mercante mundial, lo hayan firmado sin reserva en cuanto a ratificación, aceptación o aprobación o hayan depositado el pertinente instrumento de ratificación, aceptación, aprobación o adhesión, de conformidad con lo dispuesto en el artículo 17.

2   Para los Estados que hayan depositado un instrumento de ratificación, aceptación, aprobación o adhesión respecto del presente Convenio después de que se hayan cumplido las condiciones para su entrada en vigor pero antes de la fecha de entrada en vigor, la ratificación, aceptación, aprobación o adhesión surtirá efecto en la fecha de entrada en vigor del presente Convenio o tres meses después de la fecha de depósito del instrumento, si ésta es posterior.

3   Todo instrumento de ratificación, aceptación, aprobación o adhesión depositado después de la fecha en que el presente Convenio entre en vigor surtirá efecto tres meses después de la fecha de su depósito.

4   Después de la fecha en que una enmienda al presente Convenio se considere aceptada en virtud del artículo 19, todo instrumento de ratificación, aceptación, aprobación o adhesión depositado se aplicará al presente Convenio enmendado.

Artículo 19
Enmiendas

1   El presente Convenio podrá enmendarse mediante cualquiera de los procedimientos especificados a continuación.

2   Enmienda previo examen por la Organización:

a)   Todas las Partes podrán proponer enmiendas al presente Convenio. Las propuestas de enmiendas se presentarán al Secretario General, que las distribuirá a las Partes y a los Miembros de la Organización por lo menos seis meses antes de su examen.

b)   Toda enmienda propuesta y distribuida de conformidad con este procedimiento se remitirá al Comité para su examen. Las Partes, sean o no Miembros de la Organización, tendrán derecho a participar en las deliberaciones del Comité a efectos del examen y adopción de la enmienda.

c)   Las enmiendas se adoptarán por una mayoría de dos tercios de las Partes presentes y votantes en el Comité, a condición de que al menos un tercio de las Partes esté presente en el momento de la votación.

d)   El Secretario General comunicará a las Partes las enmiendas adoptadas de conformidad con el apartado c) para su aceptación.

e)   Una enmienda se considerará aceptada en las siguientes circunstancias:

   i)   Una enmienda a un artículo del presente Convenio se considerará aceptada en la fecha en que dos tercios de las Partes hayan notificado al Secretario General que la aceptan.

   ii)   Una enmienda al anexo se considerará aceptada cuando hayan transcurrido doce meses desde la fecha de su adopción o cualquier otra fecha que decida el Comité. No obstante, si antes de esa fecha más de un tercio de las Partes notifican al Secretario General objeciones a la enmienda, se considerará que ésta no ha sido aceptada.

f) Una enmienda entrará en vigor en las siguientes condiciones:

    i) Una enmienda a un artículo del presente Convenio entrará en vigor para aquellas Partes que hayan declarado que la aceptan seis meses después de la fecha en que se considere aceptada de conformidad con lo dispuesto en el inciso e) i).

    ii) Una enmienda al anexo entrará en vigor con respecto a todas las Partes seis meses después de la fecha en que se considere aceptada, excepto para las Partes que hayan:

        1) notificado su objeción a la enmienda de conformidad con lo dispuesto en el inciso e) ii) y no hayan retirado tal objeción; o

        2) notificado al Secretario General, antes de la entrada en vigor de dicha enmienda, que la enmienda sólo entrará en vigor para ellas una vez que hayan notificado que la aceptan.

g) i) Una Parte que haya notificado una objeción con arreglo a lo dispuesto en el inciso f) ii) 1) puede notificar posteriormente al Secretario General que acepta la enmienda. Dicha enmienda entrará en vigor para la Parte en cuestión seis meses después de la fecha en que haya notificado su aceptación, o de la fecha en la que la enmienda entre en vigor, si ésta es posterior.

    ii) En el caso de que una Parte que haya hecho una notificación en virtud de lo dispuesto en el inciso f) ii) 2) notifique al Secretario General que acepta una enmienda, dicha enmienda entrará en vigor para la Parte en cuestión seis meses después de la fecha en que haya notificado su aceptación, o de la fecha en la que la enmienda entre en vigor, si ésta es posterior.

3 Enmienda mediante Conferencia:

a) A solicitud de cualquier Parte, y siempre que concuerde en ello un tercio cuando menos de las Partes, la Organización convocará una conferencia de las Partes para examinar enmiendas al presente Convenio.

b) Toda enmienda adoptada en tal conferencia por una mayoría de dos tercios de las Partes presentes y votantes será comunicada por el Secretario General a todas las Partes para su aceptación.

c) Salvo que la conferencia decida otra cosa, la enmienda se considerará aceptada y entrará en vigor de conformidad con los procedimientos especificados en los apartados 2 e) y 2 f), respectivamente.

4 Toda Parte que haya rehusado aceptar una enmienda al anexo no será considerada como Parte a los efectos de la aplicación de esa enmienda, exclusivamente.

5 Toda notificación que se haga en virtud del presente artículo se presentará por escrito al Secretario General.

6 El Secretario General informará a las Partes y a los Miembros de la Organización de:

a) toda enmienda que entre en vigor, y de su fecha de entrada en vigor, en general y para cada Parte en particular; y

b) toda notificación hecha en virtud del presente artículo.

Artículo 20
Denuncia

1 El presente Convenio podrá ser denunciado por cualquier Parte en cualquier momento posterior a la expiración de un plazo de dos años a contar desde la fecha en que el presente Convenio haya entrado en vigor para esa Parte.

2 La denuncia se efectuará mediante notificación por escrito al depositario para que surta efecto un año después de su recepción o al expirar cualquier otro plazo más largo que se indique en dicha notificación.

Artículo 21
Depositario

1 El presente Convenio será depositado ante el Secretario General, quien remitirá copias certificadas del mismo a todos los Estados que lo hayan firmado o se hayan adherido a él.

2 Además de desempeñar las funciones especificadas en otras partes del presente Convenio, el Secretario General:

a) informará a todos los Estados que hayan firmado el presente Convenio o se hayan adherido al mismo de:

i) toda nueva firma o depósito de un instrumento de ratificación, aceptación, aprobación o adhesión, así como de la fecha en que se produzca;

ii) la fecha de entrada en vigor del presente Convenio; y

iii) todo instrumento de denuncia del presente Convenio que se deposite, así como de la fecha en que se recibió dicho instrumento y la fecha en que la denuncia surtirá efecto; y

b) tan pronto como el presente Convenio entre en vigor, remitirá el texto del mismo a la Secretaría de las Naciones Unidas a efectos de registro y publicación de conformidad con el Artículo 102 de la Carta de las Naciones Unidas.

Artículo 22
Idiomas

El presente Convenio está redactado en un solo original en los idiomas árabe, chino, español, francés, inglés y ruso, siendo cada uno de esos textos igualmente auténtico.

HECHO EN LONDRES el día trece de febrero de dos mil cuatro.

EN FE DE LO CUAL los infrascritos*, debidamente autorizados al efecto por sus respectivos Gobiernos, han firmado el presente Convenio.

---

* Se omiten las firmas.

Anexo
Reglas para el control y la gestión del agua de lastre y los sedimentos de los buques

SECCIÓN A – DISPOSICIONES GENERALES

Regla A-1
Definiciones

A los efectos del presente anexo:

1 Por *fecha de vencimiento anual* se entiende el día y el mes de cada año correspondientes a la fecha de expiración del Certificado.

2 Por *capacidad de agua de lastre* se entiende la capacidad volumétrica total de todo tanque, espacio o compartimiento de un buque que se utilice para el transporte, la carga o descarga del agua de lastre, incluido cualquier tanque, espacio o compartimiento multiusos proyectado para poder transportar agua de lastre.

3 Por *compañía* se entiende el propietario del buque o cualquier otra organización o persona, tal como el gestor naval o el arrendatario a casco desnudo, que haya asumido la responsabilidad del propietario del buque de su funcionamiento y que, al asumir tal responsabilidad, ha aceptado asumir todas las funciones y responsabilidades impuestas por el Código Internacional de Gestión de la Seguridad[*].

4 Por *construido* con referencia a un buque se entiende una fase de construcción en la que:

    .1 la quilla ha sido colocada; o

    .2 comienza la construcción que puede identificarse como propia de un buque concreto; o

    .3 ha comenzado, respecto del buque de que se trate, el montaje que supone la utilización de cuando menos 50 toneladas del total estimado de material estructural o un uno por ciento de dicho total, si este segundo valor es menor; o

    .4 el buque es objeto de una transformación importante.

5 Por *transformación importante* se entiende la transformación de un buque que:

---

[*] Véase el Código IGS, adoptado por la Organización mediante la resolución A.714(18), en su forma enmendada.

.1 modifica su capacidad de transporte de agua de lastre en un porcentaje igual o superior al 15 %; o

.2 supone un cambio del tipo de buque; o

.3 a juicio de la Administración, está destinada a prolongar la vida del buque en diez años o más; o

.4 tiene como resultado modificaciones de su sistema de agua de lastre no consistentes en una sustitución de componentes por otros del mismo tipo. No se considerará que la transformación de un buque existente para que cumpla las disposiciones de la regla D-1 constituye una transformación importante a efectos del presente anexo.

6 Por la expresión *de la tierra más próxima* se entiende desde la línea de base a partir de la cual queda establecido el mar territorial del territorio de que se trate de conformidad con el derecho internacional, con la salvedad de que, a los efectos del presente Convenio, a lo largo de la costa nordeste de Australia, *de la tierra más próxima* significará desde una línea trazada a partir de un punto de la costa australiana situado en latitud 11°00′ S, longitud 142°08′ E, hasta un punto de latitud 10°35′ S, longitud 141°55′ E, desde allí a un punto en latitud 10°00′ S, longitud 142°00′ E, y luego sucesivamente a

latitud 9°10′ S, longitud 143°52′ E
latitud 9°00′ S, longitud 144°30′ E
latitud 10°41′ S, longitud 145°00′ E
latitud 13°00′ S, longitud 145°00′ E
latitud 15°00′ S, longitud 146°00′ E
latitud 17°30′ S, longitud 147°00′ E
latitud 21°00′ S, longitud 152°55′ E
latitud 24°30′ S, longitud 154°00′ E
y finalmente, desde esta posición
hasta un punto de la costa de Australia
en latitud 24°42′ S, longitud 153°15′ E.

7 Por *sustancia activa* se entiende una sustancia u organismo, incluido un virus o un hongo, que ejerza una acción general o específica contra los organismos acuáticos perjudiciales y agentes patógenos.

Regla A-2
Aplicación general

Salvo indicación expresa en otro sentido, la descarga del agua de lastre sólo se realizará mediante la gestión del agua de lastre de conformidad con las disposiciones del presente anexo.

Regla A-3
Excepciones

Las prescripciones de la regla B-3, o cualquier medida adoptada por una Parte en virtud del artículo 2.3 o de la sección C, no se aplicarán a:

.1 la toma o descarga de agua de lastre y sedimentos necesaria para garantizar la seguridad del buque en situaciones de emergencia o salvar vidas humanas en el mar;

.2 la descarga o entrada accidental de agua de lastre y sedimentos ocasionada por la avería de un buque o de su equipo:

.1 siempre que antes y después de que haya tenido lugar la avería o se haya descubierto ésta o la descarga se hayan tomado todas las precauciones razonables para evitar o reducir al mínimo la descarga; y

.2 a menos que el propietario, la compañía o el oficial a cargo hayan ocasionado la avería de forma intencionada o temeraria;

.3 la toma o descarga de agua de lastre y sedimentos que se realice con el propósito de evitar sucesos de contaminación debidos al buque o reducir al mínimo las consecuencias de éstos;

.4 la toma y posterior descarga en alta mar de la misma agua de lastre y sedimentos;

.5 la descarga del agua de lastre y los sedimentos de un buque en el mismo lugar del que proceda la totalidad de esa agua de lastre y esos sedimentos, siempre que no haya habido mezcla con agua de lastre o sedimentos sin gestionar procedentes de otras zonas. Si ha habido mezcla, el agua de lastre tomada de otras zonas estará sujeta a la gestión del agua de lastre de conformidad con el presente anexo.

Regla A-4
Exenciones

1 Una Parte o Partes podrán conceder, en las aguas bajo su jurisdicción, exenciones con respecto a cualquier prescripción de aplicar las reglas B-3 o C-1, además de las que figuran en otras disposiciones del presente Convenio, pero sólo cuando tales exenciones:

.1 se concedan a un buque o buques que realicen un viaje o viajes entre puertos o lugares específicos; o a un buque que opere exclusivamente entre puertos o lugares específicos;

.2 sean efectivas por un periodo no superior a cinco años, a reserva de un examen intermedio;

.3 se concedan a buques que no mezclen agua de lastre ni sedimentos excepto entre los puertos o lugares especificados en el párrafo 1.1; y

.4 se concedan de conformidad con las directrices sobre la evaluación de riesgos elaboradas por la Organización.

2 Las exenciones concedidas en virtud del párrafo 1 no serán efectivas hasta después de haberlas comunicado a la Organización y haberse distribuido la información pertinente a las Partes.

3   Toda exención concedida en virtud de la presente regla no dañará ni deteriorará el medio ambiente, la salud de los seres humanos, los bienes o los recursos de los Estados adyacentes o de otros Estados. Se mantendrán las pertinentes consultas con todo Estado que una Parte determine que puede resultar perjudicado con miras a resolver cualquier preocupación identificada.

4   Toda exención concedida en virtud de la presente regla se anotará en el Libro registro del agua de lastre.

Regla A-5
Cumplimiento equivalente

En el caso de las embarcaciones de recreo utilizadas exclusivamente para ocio o competiciones o las embarcaciones utilizadas principalmente para búsqueda y salvamento, de eslora total inferior a 50 m y con una capacidad máxima de agua de lastre de ocho metros cúbicos, el cumplimiento equivalente del presente anexo será determinado por la Administración, teniendo en cuenta las directrices elaboradas por la Organización.

SECCIÓN B – PRESCRIPCIONES DE GESTIÓN Y CONTROL APLICABLES A LOS BUQUES

Regla B-1
Plan de gestión del agua de lastre

Cada buque llevará a bordo y aplicará un plan de gestión del agua de lastre. Dicho plan estará aprobado por la Administración teniendo en cuenta las directrices elaboradas por la Organización. El plan de gestión del agua de lastre será específico de cada buque y, como mínimo:

   .1   indicará de forma detallada los procedimientos de seguridad para el buque y la tripulación relativos a la gestión del agua de lastre prescrita por el presente Convenio;

   .2   ofrecerá una descripción detallada de las medidas que han de adoptarse para implantar las prescripciones sobre gestión del agua de lastre y las respectivas prácticas complementarias indicadas en el presente Convenio;

   .3   indicará de forma detallada los procedimientos para la evacuación de los sedimentos:

       .1   en el mar; y

       .2   en tierra;

   .4   incluirá los procedimientos para coordinar la gestión del agua de lastre a bordo que incluya la descarga en el mar con las autoridades del Estado en cuyas aguas tengan lugar las descargas;

.5 contendrá el nombre del oficial de a bordo encargado de velar por la aplicación correcta del plan;

.6 incluirá las prescripciones de notificación previstas para los buques en el presente Convenio; y

.7 estará redactado en el idioma de trabajo del buque. Si el idioma utilizado no es el español, el francés ni el inglés, se incluirá una traducción a uno de esos idiomas.

Regla B-2
Libro registro del agua de lastre

1   Cada buque llevará a bordo un Libro registro del agua de lastre, que podrá ser un sistema electrónico de registro, o que podrá estar integrado en otro libro o sistema de registro, y que contendrá como mínimo la información especificada en el apéndice II.

2   Los asientos del Libro registro del agua de lastre se mantendrán a bordo del buque durante dos años, como mínimo, después de efectuado el último asiento, y posteriormente permanecerán en poder de la compañía por un plazo mínimo de tres años.

3   En caso de efectuarse una descarga del agua de lastre de conformidad con las reglas A-3, A-4 o B-3.6, o de producirse una descarga accidental o excepcional cuya exención no esté contemplada en el presente Convenio, se hará una anotación en el Libro registro del agua de lastre que indicará las circunstancias de tal descarga y las razones que llevaron a la misma.

4   El Libro registro del agua de lastre se guardará de forma que sea posible su inspección en cualquier momento razonable y, en el caso de un buque sin dotación que esté siendo remolcado, podrá conservarse a bordo del remolcador.

5   Cada una de las operaciones relacionadas con la gestión del agua de lastre se anotará inmediatamente con todos sus pormenores en el Libro registro del agua de lastre. Cada asiento será firmado por el oficial o los oficiales a cargo de la operación de que se trate, y cada página debidamente cumplimentada será refrendada por el capitán. Los asientos del Libro registro del agua de lastre se harán en uno de los idiomas de trabajo del buque. Si el idioma utilizado no es el español, el francés ni el inglés, el texto irá acompañado de una traducción a uno de esos idiomas. Cuando se utilicen también asientos redactados en un idioma nacional oficial del Estado cuyo pabellón tenga derecho a enarbolar el buque, dichos asientos darán fe en caso de controversia o discrepancia.

6   Los oficiales debidamente autorizados por una Parte estarán facultados para inspeccionar el Libro registro del agua de lastre a bordo de cualquier buque al que se aplique la presente regla mientras dicho buque esté en uno de sus puertos o terminales mar adentro, y podrán sacar copia de cualquier asiento y solicitar al capitán que certifique que es una copia auténtica. Toda copia certificada será admitida en cualquier procedimiento judicial como prueba de los hechos declarados en el asiento. La inspección del Libro registro del agua de lastre y la extracción de copias certificadas se harán con toda la diligencia posible y sin causar demoras innecesarias al buque.

Regla B-3
Gestión del agua de lastre de los buques

1   Los buques construidos antes de 2009:

   .1   con una capacidad de agua de lastre comprendida entre 1 500 y 5 000 m^3, inclusive, habrán de llevar a cabo una gestión del agua de lastre que cumpla como mínimo la norma descrita en la regla D-1 o bien en la regla D-2 hasta 2014, fecha después de la cual habrá de cumplir como mínimo la norma descrita en la regla D-2;

   .2   con una capacidad de agua de lastre inferior a 1 500 m^3 o superior a 5 000 habrán de llevar a cabo una gestión del agua de lastre que cumpla como mínimo la norma descrita en la regla D-1 o bien en la regla D-2 hasta 2016, fecha después de la cual habrá de cumplir como mínimo la norma descrita en la regla D-2.

2   Los buques a los que se aplique el párrafo 1 cumplirán lo dispuesto en el mismo a más tardar en el primer reconocimiento intermedio, o de renovación, si éste es anterior, tras la fecha de aniversario de la entrega del buque en el año de cumplimiento de la norma aplicable a dicho buque.

3   Los buques construidos en 2009 o posteriormente que tengan una capacidad de agua de lastre inferior a 5 000 m^3 habrán de llevar a cabo una gestión del agua de lastre que cumpla como mínimo la norma descrita en la regla D-2.

4   Los buques construidos en 2009 o posteriormente, pero antes de 2012, que tengan una capacidad de agua de lastre igual o superior a 5 000 m^3 habrán de llevar a cabo una gestión del agua de lastre conforme a lo dispuesto en el párrafo 1.2.

5   Los buques construidos en 2012 o posteriormente que tengan una capacidad de agua de lastre igual o superior a 5 000 m^3 habrán de llevar a cabo una gestión del agua de lastre que cumpla como mínimo la norma descrita en la regla D-2.

6   Las prescripciones de la presente regla no son aplicables a los buques que descarguen el agua de lastre en instalaciones de recepción proyectadas teniendo en cuenta las directrices elaboradas por la Organización para tales instalaciones.

7   Podrán aceptarse también otros métodos de gestión del agua de lastre diferentes a los prescritos en los párrafos 1 a 5, siempre que dichos métodos garanticen como mínimo el mismo grado de protección del medio ambiente, la salud de los seres humanos, los bienes o los recursos, y cuenten en principio con la aprobación del Comité.

Regla B-4
Cambio del agua de lastre

1   Los buques que lleven a cabo la gestión del agua de lastre para cumplir la norma de la regla D-1, habrán de atenerse a lo siguiente:

> **.1**   siempre que sea posible, efectuarán el cambio del agua de lastre a por lo menos 200 millas marinas de la tierra más próxima y en aguas de 200 m de profundidad como mínimo, teniendo en cuenta las directrices elaboradas por la Organización;

> **.2**   en los casos en que el buque no pueda efectuar el cambio del agua de lastre de conformidad con lo dispuesto en el párrafo 1.1, tal cambio del agua de lastre se llevará a cabo teniendo en cuenta las directrices descritas en el párrafo 1.1 y tan lejos como sea posible de la tierra más próxima, y en todos los casos por lo menos a 50 millas marinas de la tierra más próxima y en aguas de 200 m de profundidad como mínimo;

2   En las zonas marítimas donde la distancia a la tierra más próxima o la profundidad no cumpla los parámetros descritos en los párrafos 1.1 ó 1.2, el Estado rector del puerto, en consulta con los Estados adyacentes o con otros Estados, según proceda, podrá designar zonas en las que se permita al buque efectuar el cambio del agua de lastre teniendo en cuenta las directrices descritas en el párrafo 1.1.

3   No se exigirá a un buque que se desvíe de su viaje previsto, o lo retrase, con el fin de cumplir una determinada prescripción del párrafo 1.

4   Un buque que efectúe el cambio del agua de lastre no tendrá que cumplir lo dispuesto en los párrafos 1 ó 2, según proceda, si el capitán decide razonablemente que tal cambio podría poner en peligro la seguridad o estabilidad del buque, a la tripulación o a los pasajeros por las malas condiciones meteorológicas, el proyecto o esfuerzos del buque, un fallo del equipo, o cualquier otra circunstancia extraordinaria.

5   Cuando un buque tenga que efectuar la gestión del agua de lastre y no lo haga de conformidad con la presente regla, las razones se anotarán en el Libro registro del agua de lastre.

Regla B-5
Gestión de los sedimentos de los buques

1   Todos los buques extraerán y evacuarán los sedimentos de los espacios destinados a transportar agua de lastre de conformidad con las disposiciones del plan de gestión del agua de lastre del buque.

2   Los buques descritos en las reglas B-3.3 a B-3.5 deberían proyectarse y construirse, sin comprometer la seguridad ni la eficacia operacional, con miras a que se reduzca al mínimo la toma y retención no deseable de sedimentos, se facilite la remoción de éstos y se posibilite el acceso sin riesgos para la remoción de sedimentos y el muestreo de éstos, teniendo en cuenta en las directrices elaboradas por la Organización. En la medida de lo posible, los buques descritos en la regla B-3.1 deberían cumplir lo dispuesto en el presente párrafo.

Regla B-6
Funciones de los oficiales y tripulantes

Los oficiales y tripulantes estarán familiarizados con sus funciones en relación con la gestión del agua de lastre específica del buque en el que presten sus servicios y también estarán familiarizados, en la medida en que corresponda a sus funciones, con el plan de gestión del agua de lastre del buque.

SECCIÓN C – PRESCRIPCIONES ESPECIALES PARA CIERTAS ZONAS

Regla C-1
Medidas adicionales

1   Si una Parte, individualmente o junto con otras Partes, determina que es necesario que se tomen medidas adicionales a las incluidas en la sección B, para prevenir, reducir o eliminar la transferencia de organismos acuáticos perjudiciales y agentes patógenos a través del agua de lastre y los sedimentos de los buques a zonas de su jurisdicción, dicha Parte o Partes podrán dispo-ner, de conformidad con el derecho internacional, que los buques cumplan una determinada norma o prescripción.

2   Antes de establecer normas o prescripciones en virtud del párrafo 1, la Parte o Partes deberían consultar a los Estados adyacentes o a otros Estados a los que puedan afectar tales normas o prescripciones.

3   La Parte o Partes que tengan la intención de introducir medidas adicionales de conformidad con lo dispuesto en el párrafo 1:

   .1   tendrán en cuenta las directrices elaboradas por la Organización;

   .2   comunicarán dicha intención de establecer una medida o medidas adicionales a la Organización al menos seis meses antes de la fecha prevista de implantación de tal o tales medidas, salvo en situaciones de emergencia o de epidemia. Dicha comunicación incluirá:

      .1   las coordenadas exactas de la zona de aplicación de tal medida o medidas adicionales;

      .2   la necesidad y las razones que justifican la aplicación de la medida o medidas adicionales, incluidos sus beneficios cuando sea posible;

      .3   una descripción de la medida o medidas adicionales; y

      .4   toda disposición que pudiera adoptarse para facilitar a los buques el cumplimiento de la medida o medidas adicionales;

.3 obtendrán la aprobación de la Organización en la medida en que lo exija el derecho internacional consuetudinario recogido en la Convención de las Naciones Unidas sobre el Derecho del Mar, según proceda.

4 La Parte o Partes que introduzcan tales medidas adicionales procurarán facilitar todos los servicios correspondientes, lo que puede incluir, sin limitarse a ello, la notificación a los navegantes de las zonas disponibles y de las rutas o puertos alternativos, en la medida de lo posible, con el fin de aligerar la carga para el buque.

5 Cualquier medida adicional que adopten una Parte o Partes no comprometerá la seguridad ni la protección del buque y bajo ninguna circunstancia entrará en conflicto con otros convenios que el buque tenga que cumplir.

6 La Parte o Partes que introduzcan medidas adicionales podrán eximir del cumplimiento de tales medidas durante un determinado periodo de tiempo o en circunstancias concretas, según consideren oportuno.

Regla C-2
Avisos sobre la toma de agua de lastre en ciertas zonas y medidas conexas del Estado de abanderamiento

1 Las Partes se esforzarán por notificar a los navegantes las zonas bajo su jurisdicción en las que los buques no deberían tomar agua de lastre por existir en ellas condiciones conocidas. Las Partes incluirán en tales avisos las coordenadas exactas de la zona o zonas en cuestión y, de ser posible, la situación de toda zona o zonas alternativas para la toma de agua de lastre. Se podrán emitir avisos para las zonas:

.1 en las que se sepa que existen brotes, infestaciones o poblaciones de organismos acuáticos perjudiciales y agentes patógenos (por ejemplo, proliferación de algas tóxicas) que probablemente afecten a la toma o descarga de agua de lastre;

.2 en cuyas cercanías haya desagües de aguas residuales; o

.3 en las que la dispersión mareal sea deficiente o en las que haya veces en que se sepa que una corriente mareal presenta más turbiedad.

2 Además de informar a los navegantes sobre estas zonas conforme a lo dispuesto en el párrafo 1, las Partes informarán a la Organización y a todo Estado ribereño que pudiera verse afectado de cualesquiera zonas identificadas en el párrafo 1, indicando el periodo de tiempo durante el cual tal aviso permanecerá probablemente en vigor. El aviso a la Organización y a todo Estado ribereño que pudiere verse afectado incluirá las coordenadas exactas de la zona o zonas y, allí donde sea posible, la situación de toda zona o zonas alternativas para la toma de agua de lastre. El aviso incluirá un asesoramiento para los buques que necesiten tomar agua de lastre en la zona y describirá las medidas alternativas para el suministro. Las Partes notificarán

también a los navegantes, a la Organización y a todo Estado ribereño que pudiera verse afectado el momento a partir del cual un determinado aviso dejará de estar en vigor.

Regla C-3
Comunicación de información

La Organización dará a conocer, por los medios apropiados, la información que se le haya comunicado en virtud de las reglas C-1 y C-2.

SECCIÓN D – NORMAS PARA LA GESTIÓN DEL AGUA DE LASTRE

Regla D-1
Norma para el cambio del agua de lastre

1   Los buques que efectúen el cambio del agua de lastre de conformidad con la presente regla lo harán con una eficacia del 95%, como mínimo, de cambio volumétrico del agua de lastre.

2   En el caso de los buques que cambien el agua de lastre siguiendo el método del flujo continuo, el bombeo de tres veces el volumen de cada tanque de agua de lastre se considerará conforme a la norma descrita en el párrafo 1. Se podrá aceptar un bombeo inferior a tres veces ese volumen siempre y cuando el buque pueda demostrar que se ha alcanzado el 95% de cambio volumétrico del agua de lastre.

Regla D-2
Norma de eficacia de la gestión del agua de lastre

1   Los buques que efectúen la gestión del agua de lastre conforme a lo dispuesto en la presente regla descargarán menos de 10 organismos viables por metro cúbico cuyo tamaño mínimo sea igual o superior a 50 micras y menos de 10 organismos viables por mililitro cuyo tamaño mínimo sea inferior a 50 micras e igual o superior a 10 micras; además, la descarga de los microbios indicadores no excederá de las concentraciones especificadas en el párrafo 2.

2   Los microbios indicadores, a efectos de la salud de los seres humanos, comprenderán los siguientes organismos:

- **.1**   *Vibrio cholerae* toxicógeno (O1 y O139): menos de 1 unidad formadora de colonias (ufc) por 100 mililitros o menos de 1 ufc por gramo (peso húmedo) de muestras de zooplancton;

- **.2**   *Escherichia coli*: menos de 250 ufc por 100 mililitros;

- **.3**   Enterococos intestinales: menos de 100 ufc por 100 mililitros.

Regla D-3
Prescripciones relativas a la aprobación
de los sistemas de gestión del agua de lastre

1	Excepto por lo especificado en el párrafo 2, los sistemas de gestión del agua de lastre utilizados para cumplir lo dispuesto en el presente Convenio estarán aprobados por la Administración de conformidad con las directrices elaboradas por la Organización.

2	Los sistemas de gestión del agua de lastre en los que se utilicen sustancias activas o preparados que contengan una o varias sustancias activas para cumplir lo dispuesto en el presente Convenio deberán ser aprobados por la Organización con arreglo a un procedimiento elaborado por la propia Organización. Este procedimiento incluirá tanto la aprobación de sustancias activas como la revocación de dicha aprobación y la forma de aplicación prevista para tales sustancias. En los casos en que se revoque una aprobación, el uso de la sustancia o sustancias activas en cuestión quedará prohibido en el plazo de un año a contar desde la fecha de dicha revocación.

3	Los sistemas de gestión del agua de lastre utilizados para cumplir lo dispuesto en el presente Convenio deberán ser seguros para el buque, su equipo y su tripulación.

Regla D-4
Prototipos de tecnologías de tratamiento
del agua de lastre

1	A los buques que con anterioridad a la fecha en que entraría en vigor para ellos la norma descrita en la regla D-2 participen en un programa aprobado por la Administración para poner a prueba y evaluar tecnologías de tratamiento del agua de lastre prometedoras, no les será aplicable dicha norma hasta que hayan transcurrido cinco años desde la fecha en la que, de no ser así, tendrían que haber empezado a cumplir tal norma.

2	A los buques que con posterioridad a la fecha de entrada en vigor para ellos de la norma descrita en la regla D-2 participen en un programa aprobado por la Administración, teniendo en cuenta las directrices elaboradas por la Organización, para poner a prueba y evaluar tecnologías de tratamiento del agua de lastre prometedoras, y que tenga posibilidades de llegar a ofrecer tecnologías de un nivel superior al de la norma descrita en la regla D-2, se les dejará de aplicar esta norma durante cinco años, a contar desde la fecha de instalación de tal tecnología.

3	Para el establecimiento y ejecución de cualquier programa de prueba y evaluación de tecnologías de tratamiento del agua de lastre prometedoras, las Partes:

.1	tendrán en cuenta las directrices elaboradas por la Organización, y

.2	sólo permitirán participar al número mínimo de buques necesario para probar efectivamente tales tecnologías.

4   Durante todo el periodo de prueba y evaluación, el sistema de tratamiento se utilizará de manera regular y con arreglo a lo proyectado.

Regla D-5
Examen de normas por la Organización

1   En una reunión del Comité que se celebrará a más tardar tres años antes de la fecha más temprana de entrada en vigor de la norma descrita en la regla D-2, el Comité llevará a cabo un examen que, entre otras cosas, determine si se dispone de las tecnologías adecuadas para el cumplimiento de dicha norma y evalúe los criterios del párrafo 2 y las repercusiones socioeconómicas específicamente en relación con las necesidades de desarrollo de los países en desarrollo, especialmente de los pequeños Estados insulares en desarrollo. El Comité también realizará los exámenes periódicos que sean pertinentes sobre las prescripciones aplicables a los buques descritas en la regla B-3.1, así como sobre cualesquiera otros aspectos de la gestión del agua de lastre tratados en el presente anexo, incluidas las directrices elaboradas por la Organización.

2   En dichos exámenes de las tecnologías adecuadas deberán tenerse en cuenta asimismo:

   .1 los aspectos relacionados con la seguridad del buque y la tripulación;

   .2 su aceptabilidad desde el punto de vista ambiental, es decir, que no causen más o mayores problemas ambientales de los que resuelven;

   .3 su aspecto práctico, es decir que sean compatibles con el funcionamiento y el proyecto de los buques;

   .4 su eficacia en función de los costos, es decir, los aspectos económicos; y

   .5 su eficacia desde el punto de vista biológico para eliminar o hacer inviables los organismos acuáticos perjudiciales y agentes patógenos del agua de lastre.

3   El Comité podrá constituir un grupo o grupos para que lleven a cabo el examen o exámenes descritos en el párrafo 1. El Comité determinará la composición, el mandato y las cuestiones específicas que habrá de tratar cualquier grupo que se constituya. Tales grupos podrán elaborar y recomendar propuestas de enmienda del presente anexo para que las examinen las Partes. Sólo las Partes podrán participar en la formulación de recomendaciones y en las decisiones sobre enmiendas que adopte el Comité.

4   Si, basándose en los exámenes descritos en la presente regla, las Partes deciden adoptar enmiendas al presente anexo, tales enmiendas se adoptarán y entrarán en vigor de conformidad con los procedimientos que figuran en el artículo 19 del presente Convenio.

SECCIÓN E – PRESCRIPCIONES SOBRE RECONOCIMIENTOS Y CERTIFICACIÓN PARA LA GESTIÓN DEL AGUA DE LASTRE

Regla E-1
Reconocimientos

1   Los buques de arqueo bruto igual o superior a 400 a los que se aplique el presente Convenio, excluidas las plataformas flotantes, las UFA y las unidades FPAD, serán objeto de los reconocimientos que se especifican a continuación:

> **.1**   un reconocimiento inicial antes de que el buque entre en servicio o de que se expida por primera vez el Certificado prescrito en las reglas E-2 o E-3. Este reconocimiento verificará que el plan de gestión del agua de lastre exigido en la regla B-1 y la estructura, el equipo, los sistemas, los accesorios, los medios y los materiales o procedimientos conexos cumplen plenamente las prescripciones del presente Convenio;

> **.2**   un reconocimiento de renovación a intervalos especificados por la Administración, pero que no excedan de cinco años, salvo cuando sean aplicables las reglas E-5.2, E-5.5, E-5.6 o E-5.7. Este reconocimiento verificará que el plan de gestión del agua de lastre exigido en la regla B-1 y la estructura, el equipo, los sistemas, los accesorios, los medios y los materiales o procedimientos conexos cumplen plenamente las prescripciones aplicables del presente Convenio;

> **.3**   un reconocimiento intermedio dentro de los tres meses anteriores o posteriores a la segunda fecha de vencimiento anual, o dentro de los tres meses anteriores o posteriores a la tercera fecha de vencimiento anual del Certificado, que sustituirá a uno de los reconocimientos anuales especificados en el párrafo 1.4. El reconocimiento intermedio será tal que garantice que el equipo y los sistemas y procedimientos conexos de gestión del agua de lastre cumplen plenamente las prescripciones aplicables del presente anexo y funcionan debidamente. Tales reconocimientos intermedios se refrendarán en el Certificado expedido en virtud de las reglas E-2 o E-3;

> **.4**   un reconocimiento anual dentro de los tres meses anteriores o posteriores a la fecha de vencimiento anual del Certificado, incluida una inspección general de toda estructura, equipo, sistemas, accesorios, medios y materiales o procedimientos relacionados con el plan de gestión del agua de lastre exigido en la regla B-1, para garantizar que se han mantenido de conformidad con lo estipulado en el párrafo 9 y que siguen siendo satisfactorios para el servicio al que está destinado el buque. Tales

reconocimientos anuales se refrendarán en el Certificado expedido en virtud de las reglas E-2 o E-3;

.5 se efectuará un reconocimiento adicional, ya sea general o parcial, según dicten las circunstancias, después de haberse efectuado una modificación, una sustitución o una reparación importante en la estructura, el equipo, los sistemas, los accesorios, los medios y los materiales, necesaria para lograr el pleno cumplimiento del presente Convenio. El reconocimiento será tal que garantice que tal modificación, sustitución o reparación importante se ha realizado efectivamente para que el buque cumpla las prescripciones del presente Convenio. Tales reconocimientos se refrendarán en el Certificado expedido en virtud de lo dispuesto en las reglas E-2 o E-3.

2 Respecto de los buques que no estén sujetos a lo dispuesto en el párrafo 1, la Administración dictará las medidas apropiadas para garantizar el cumplimiento de las disposiciones aplicables del presente Convenio.

3 Los reconocimientos de los buques para hacer cumplir las disposiciones del presente Convenio serán realizados por funcionarios de la Administración. No obstante, la Administración podrá confiar los reconocimientos a inspectores designados al efecto o a organizaciones reconocidas por ella.

4 Una Administración que, según se describe en el párrafo 3, designe inspectores o reconozca organizaciones para realizar los reconocimientos facultará a tales inspectores designados u organizaciones reconocidas* para que, como mínimo, puedan:

.1 exigir a los buques que inspeccionen que cumplan las prescripciones del presente Convenio; y

.2 realizar reconocimientos e inspecciones cuando se lo soliciten las autoridades competentes de un Estado rector de puerto que sea Parte.

5 La Administración notificará a la Organización las responsabilidades concretas y las condiciones de la autoridad delegada en los inspectores designados o las organizaciones reconocidas a fin de que se comuniquen a las Partes para información de sus funcionarios.

6 Cuando la Administración, un inspector designado o una organización reconocida determinen que la gestión del agua de lastre del buque no se ajusta a las especificaciones del Certificado exigido en virtud de las reglas E-2 o E-3, o es tal que el buque no es apto para hacerse a la mar sin que represente un riesgo para el medio ambiente, la salud de los seres humanos, los bienes o los recursos, tal inspector u organización se asegurarán inmediatamente de que se adoptan medidas correctivas con objeto de que el buque cumpla lo dispuesto. Se informará inmediatamente a un inspector u organización, que se asegurará de que el Certificado se retira o no se expide, según sea el caso. Si el buque se encuentra en un puerto de otra Parte, el

---

* Véanse las directrices adoptadas por la Organización mediante la resolución A.739(18), según sean enmendadas por la Organización, y las especificaciones adoptadas por la Organización mediante la resolución A.789(18), según sean enmendadas por la Organiación.

hecho se notificará inmediatamente a las autoridades competentes del Estado rector del puerto. Cuando un funcionario de la Administración, un inspector designado o una organización reconocida hayan notificado el hecho a las autoridades competentes del Estado rector del puerto, el Gobierno de dicho Estado prestará al funcionario, inspector u organización toda la ayuda necesaria para que pueda cumplir sus obligaciones en virtud de la presente regla, incluidas las medidas descritas en el artículo 9.

7   Siempre que un buque sufra un accidente o se descubra en un buque algún defecto que afecte seriamente a su capacidad para realizar la gestión del agua de lastre de conformidad con lo prescrito en el presente Convenio, el propietario, el armador u otra persona que tenga el buque a su cargo informará lo antes posible a la Administración, a la organización reconocida o al inspector designado encargados de expedir el Certificado pertinente, quienes harán que se inicien las investigaciones necesarias para determinar si es preciso realizar el reconocimiento prescrito en el párrafo 1. Cuando el buque se encuentre en un puerto de otra Parte, el propietario, el armador u otra persona que tenga el buque a su cargo informarán también inmediatamente a las autoridades competentes del Estado rector del puerto, y el inspector designado o la organización reconocida comprobarán que se ha transmitido esa información.

8   En todos los casos, la Administración interesada garantizará plenamente la integridad y eficacia del reconocimiento y se comprometerá a hacer que se tomen las disposiciones necesarias para dar cumplimiento a esta obligación.

9   El buque y su equipo, sistemas y procedimientos se mantendrán en condiciones que cumplan lo dispuesto en el presente Convenio a fin de que el buque siga siendo apto, en todos los aspectos, para hacerse a la mar sin que ello represente un riesgo para el medio ambiente, la salud de los seres humanos, los bienes o los recursos.

10   Después de terminarse cualquier reconocimiento realizado en virtud de lo dispuesto en el párrafo 1, el buque no sufrirá modificaciones de su estructura, equipo, accesorios, medios ni materiales relacionados con el plan de gestión del agua de lastre exigido en la regla B-1 e inspeccionados en ese reconocimiento, sin que la Administración haya expedido para ello la debida autorización, salvo que se trate de la sustitución de tales equipos o accesorios por otros iguales.

Regla E-2
Expedición o refrendo del Certificado

1   La Administración se asegurará de que a todo buque al que sea aplicable la regla E-1 se le expida un Certificado una vez que se haya completado satisfactoriamente un reconocimiento con arreglo a lo dispuesto en la regla E-1. Todo Certificado expedido bajo la autoridad de una Parte será aceptado por las otras Partes y tendrá, a todos los efectos del presente Convenio, la misma validez que un Certificado expedido por ellas.

2   Los Certificados serán expedidos o refrendados por la Administración, o por cualquier persona u organización debidamente autorizada por ella. En todos los casos, la Administración asume la plena responsabilidad de los Certificados.

Regla E-3
Expedición o refrendo del Certificado por otra Parte

1   A petición de la Administración, otra Parte podrá ordenar el reconocimiento de un buque y, si considera que éste cumple las disposiciones del presente Convenio, dicha Parte expedirá o autorizará la expedición de un Certificado al buque en cuestión y, cuando corresponda, refrendará o autorizará el refrendo de dicho Certificado, de conformidad con las disposiciones del presente anexo.

2   Se remitirá lo antes posible una copia del Certificado y del informe del reconocimiento a la Administración solicitante.

3   Los Certificados expedidos a petición de una Administración contendrán una declaración en la que se señale ese particular y tendrán igual validez y reconocimiento que los expedidos por esa Administración.

4   No se expedirá un Certificado a los buques que tengan derecho a enarbolar el pabellón de un Estado que no sea Parte.

Regla E-4
Modelo del Certificado

El Certificado se extenderá en el idioma oficial de la Parte que lo expida, de forma que se ajuste al modelo que figura en el apéndice I. Si el idioma utilizado no es el español, el francés ni el inglés, el texto irá acompañado de una traducción a uno de esos idiomas.

Regla E-5
Duración y validez del Certificado

1   El Certificado se expedirá para un periodo especificado por la Administración que no excederá de cinco años.

2   En el caso de los reconocimientos de renovación:

.1   independientemente de lo dispuesto en el párrafo 1, si el reconocimiento de renovación se termina dentro de los tres meses anteriores a la fecha de expiración del Certificado existente, el nuevo Certificado será válido desde la fecha en que se termine el reconocimiento de renovación hasta una fecha que no sea posterior en más de cinco años a la fecha de expiración del Certificado existente;

.2   si el reconocimiento de renovación se termina después de la fecha de expiración del Certificado existente, el nuevo Certificado será válido desde la fecha en que se termine el reconocimiento de renovación hasta una fecha que no sea posterior en más de cinco años a la fecha de expiración del Certificado existente; y

.3 si el reconocimiento de renovación se termina más de tres meses antes de la fecha de expiración del Certificado existente, el nuevo Certificado será válido desde la fecha en que se termine el reconocimiento de renovación hasta una fecha que no sea posterior en más de cinco años a la fecha en que se haya concluido dicho reconocimiento de renovación.

3 Si se expide un Certificado para un periodo inferior a cinco años, la Administración podrá prorrogar la validez de dicho Certificado más allá de la fecha de expiración hasta cubrir el periodo máximo especificado en el párrafo 1, a condición de que se efectúen, según corresponda, los reconocimientos a que se hace referencia en la regla E-1.1.3, aplicables cuando un Certificado se expide por un periodo de cinco años.

4 Si se ha concluido un reconocimiento de renovación y no se puede expedir o depositar a bordo del buque un nuevo Certificado antes de la fecha de expiración del Certificado existente, la persona u organización autorizada por la Administración podrá refrendar el Certificado existente, y dicho Certificado se aceptará como válido durante un periodo adicional que no exceda de cinco meses, contados desde la fecha de expiración.

5 Si en la fecha de expiración del Certificado un buque no se encuentra en el puerto en que haya de someterse a reconocimiento, la Administración podrá prorrogar el periodo de validez del Certificado, pero esta prórroga sólo se concederá con el fin de que el buque pueda proseguir su viaje hasta el puerto en que haya de efectuarse el reconocimiento, y aun así únicamente en los casos en que se estime oportuno y razonable hacerlo. No se prorrogará ningún Certificado por un periodo superior a tres meses, y el buque al que se le haya concedido tal prórroga no quedará autorizado en virtud de ésta, cuando llegue al puerto en que haya de efectuarse el reconocimiento, a salir de dicho puerto sin haber obtenido previamente un nuevo Certificado. Cuando se haya concluido el reconocimiento de renovación, el nuevo Certificado será válido por un periodo que no excederá de cinco años, contados desde la fecha de expiración del Certificado existente antes de que se concediera la prórroga.

6 Todo Certificado expedido a un buque dedicado a viajes cortos que no haya sido prorrogado en virtud de las disposiciones precedentes de la presente regla podrá ser prorrogado por la Administración por un periodo de gracia no superior a un mes a partir de la fecha de expiración indicada en el mismo. Cuando haya concluido el reconocimiento de renovación, el nuevo Certificado será válido por un periodo que no excederá de cinco años, contados desde la fecha de expiración del Certificado existente antes de que se concediera la prórroga.

7 En circunstancias especiales, que determinará la Administración, la fecha de un nuevo Certificado no tiene por qué coincidir con la fecha de expiración del Certificado existente, según lo prescrito en los párrafos 2.2, 5 ó 6 de la presente regla. En tales circunstancias especiales, el nuevo Certificado será válido por un periodo que no excederá de cinco años contados desde la fecha de terminación del reconocimiento de renovación.

8   Si un reconocimiento anual se termina antes del periodo especificado en la regla E-1:

.1   la fecha de vencimiento anual que conste en el Certificado se sustituirá mediante un refrendo por una fecha que no sea posterior en más de tres meses a la fecha en la que se concluyó el reconocimiento;

.2   el siguiente reconocimiento anual o intermedio prescrito por la regla E-1 se terminará en los plazos estipulados por dicha regla, tomando como referencia la nueva fecha de vencimiento anual;

.3   la fecha de expiración podrá permanecer inalterada, a condición de que se efectúen uno o más reconocimientos anuales, según proceda, de modo que no se excedan los intervalos máximos entre reconocimientos prescritos en la regla E-1.

9   Un Certificado expedido en virtud de lo dispuesto en las reglas E-2 o E-3 perderá su validez en cualquiera de los casos siguientes:

.1   si la estructura, el equipo, los sistemas, los accesorios, los medios o los materiales necesarios para cumplir plenamente el presente Convenio son objeto de modificación, sustitución o reparación importante y el Certificado no se refrenda de conformidad con lo dispuesto en el presente anexo;

.2   si el buque cambia su pabellón por el de otro Estado. Sólo se expedirá un nuevo Certificado cuando la Parte que lo expida tenga la certeza de que el buque cumple las prescripciones de la regla E-1. En caso de que el buque haya cambiado el pabellón de una Parte por el de otra, y si se solicita en los tres meses siguientes al cambio, la Parte cuyo pabellón tenía derecho a enarbolar el buque anteriormente remitirá lo antes posible a la Administración copias de los Certificados que llevara el buque antes del cambio y, si es posible, copias de los informes de los reconocimientos pertinentes;

.3   si los reconocimientos pertinentes no se concluyen en los plazos especificados en la regla E-1.1; o

.4   si el Certificado no es refrendado de conformidad con lo dispuesto en la regla E-1.1.

Apéndice I

Modelo de certificado internacional de gestión del agua de lastre

MODELO DE CERTIFICADO INTERNACIONAL DE GESTIÓN DEL AGUA DE LASTRE

Expedido en virtud de las disposiciones del Convenio internacional para el control y la gestión del agua de lastre y los sedimentos de los buques (en adelante denominado "el Convenio") con la autoridad conferida por el Gobierno de

. . . .

(nombre oficial completo del país)

por . . . .

(nombre completo de la persona u organización competente autorizada en virtud de las disposiciones del Convenio)

Datos relativos al buque*

    Nombre del buque . . . .

    Número o letras distintivos . . . .

    Puerto de matrícula . . . .

    Arqueo bruto . . . .

    Número IMO† . . . .

    Fecha de construcción . . . .

    Capacidad de agua de lastre (en metros cúbicos) . . . .

Datos relativos al método o métodos utilizados en la gestión del agua de lastre

Método utilizado en la gestión del agua de lastre . . . .

    Fecha de instalación (si procede) . . . .

    Nombre del fabricante (si procede) . . . .

---

* Los datos relativos al buque podrán indicarse también en casillas dispuestas horizontalmente.
† Sistema de asignación de un número de la OMI a los buques para su identificación, adoptado por la Organización mediante la resolución A.600(15).

Los métodos principales utilizados en la gestión del agua de lastre son los siguientes:

☐ de conformidad con la regla D-1

☐ de conformidad con la regla D-2
(descripción) . . . .

☐ el buque está sujeto a la regla D-4

SE CERTIFICA:

1   Que el buque ha sido objeto de reconocimiento de conformidad con lo prescrito en la regla E-1 del anexo del Convenio; y

2   Que el reconocimiento ha puesto de manifiesto que la gestión del agua de lastre del buque cumple las prescripciones del anexo del Convenio.

El presente certificado es válido hasta el . . . . a reserva de que se efectúen los pertinentes reconocimientos de conformidad con la regla E-1 del anexo del Convenio.

Fecha de terminación del reconocimiento en el que se basa el presente certificado: dd/mm/aaaa

Expedido en . . . .
(lugar de expedición del certificado)

a . . . .
(fecha de expedición)   *(firma del funcionario autorizado que expide
el certificado)*

(Sello o estampilla, según corresponda, de la autoridad)

REFRENDO DE RECONOCIMIENTOS ANUALES E INTERMEDIOS

SE CERTIFICA que en el reconocimiento efectuado de conformidad con lo prescrito en la regla E-1 del anexo del Convenio se ha comprobado que el buque cumple las disposiciones pertinentes del Convenio:

Reconocimiento anual   Firmado . . . .
                (firma del funcionario autorizado)

                Lugar . . . .

                Fecha . . . .

(Sello o estampilla, según corresponda, de la autoridad)

Reconocimiento anual/intermedio* Firmado . . . .
                (firma del funcionario autorizado)

                Lugar . . . .

                Fecha . . . .

(Sello o estampilla, según corresponda, de la autoridad)

Reconocimiento anual/intermedio* **Firmado** . . . .
                (firma del funcionario autorizado)

                Lugar . . . .

                Fecha . . . .

(Sello o estampilla, según corresponda, de la autoridad)

Reconocimiento anual   Firmado . . . .
                (firma del funcionario autorizado)

                Lugar . . . .

                Fecha . . . .

(Sello o estampilla, según corresponda, de la autoridad)

---

* Táchese según proceda.

RECONOCIMIENTO ANUAL/INTERMEDIO DE CONFORMIDAD
CON LO PRESCRITO EN LA REGLA E-5.8.3

SE CERTIFICA que en el reconocimiento anual/intermedio* efectuado de conformidad con lo prescrito en la regla E-5.8.3 del anexo del Convenio, se ha comprobado que el buque cumple las disposiciones pertinentes del Convenio:

Firmado . . . .
(firma del funcionario autorizado)

Lugar . . . .

Fecha . . . .

(Sello o estampilla, según corresponda, de la autoridad)

REFRENDO PARA PRORROGAR LA VALIDEZ DEL CERTIFICADO,
SI ÉSTA ES INFERIOR A CINCO AÑOS,
CUANDO LA REGLA E-5.3 SEA APLICABLE

El buque cumple las disposiciones pertinentes del Convenio, y se aceptará el presente certificado como válido, de conformidad con lo prescrito en la regla E-5.3 del anexo del Convenio, hasta . . . .

Firmado . . . .
(firma del funcionario autorizado)

Lugar . . . .

Fecha . . . .

(Sello o estampilla, según corresponda, de la autoridad)

REFRENDO CUANDO, HABIÉNDOSE CONCLUIDO EL RECONOCIMIENTO
DE RENOVACIÓN, LA REGLA E-5.4 SEA APLICABLE

El buque cumple las disposiciones pertinentes del Convenio, y se aceptará el presente certificado como válido, de conformidad con lo prescrito en la regla E-5.4 del anexo del Convenio, hasta . . . .

Firmado . . . .
(firma del funcionario autorizado)

Lugar . . . .

Fecha . . . .

(Sello o estampilla, según corresponda, de la autoridad)

---

* Táchese según proceda.

**REFRENDO PARA PRORROGAR LA VALIDEZ DEL CERTIFICADO HASTA LA
LLEGADA AL PUERTO EN QUE HA DE HACERSE EL RECONOCIMIENTO,
O POR UN PERIODO DE GRACIA, CUANDO LAS REGLAS E-5.5
O E-5.6 SEAN APLICABLES**

El presente certificado se aceptará como válido, de conformidad con lo prescrito en la regla E-5.5 o E-5.6* del anexo del Convenio, hasta ....

Firmado ....
(firma del funcionario autorizado)

Lugar ....

Fecha ....

(Sello o estampilla, según corresponda, de la autoridad)

**REFRENDO PARA ADELANTAR LA FECHA DE VENCIMIENTO ANUAL
CUANDO LA REGLA E-5.8 SEA APLICABLE**

De conformidad con lo prescrito en la regla E-5.8 del anexo del Convenio, la nueva fecha de vencimiento anual es ....

Firmado ....
(firma del funcionario autorizado)

Lugar ....

Fecha ....

(Sello o estampilla, según corresponda, de la autoridad)

De conformidad con lo prescrito en la regla E-5.8 del anexo del Convenio, la nueva fecha de vencimiento anual es ....

Firmado ....
(firma del funcionario autorizado)

Lugar ....

Fecha ....

(Sello o estampilla, según corresponda, de la autoridad)

---

* Táchese según proceda.

Apéndice II

Modelo de libro registro del agua de lastre

CONVENIO INTERNACIONAL PARA EL CONTROL Y LA GESTIÓN
DEL AGUA DE LASTRE Y LOS SEDIMIENTOS DE LOS BUQUES

Periodo: de . . . . a . . . .

Nombre del buque . . . .

Número IMO . . . .

Arqueo bruto . . . .

Pabellón . . . .

Capacidad total de agua de lastre (en metros cúbicos) . . . .

El buque dispone de un plan de gestión del agua de lastre ☐

Diagrama del buque con indicación de la situación de los tanques de lastre:

1   Introducción

De conformidad con lo dispuesto en la regla B-2 del anexo del Convenio internacional para el control y la gestión del agua de lastre y los sedimentos de los buques se llevará un registro de cada una de las operaciones que se realicen en relación con el agua de lastre, lo cual incluye tanto las descargas en el mar como las descargas en instalaciones de recepción.

2   El agua de lastre y su gestión

Por *agua de lastre* se entiende el agua, con las materias en suspensión que contenga, cargada a bordo de un buque para controlar el asiento, la escora, el calado, la estabilidad y los esfuerzos del buque. La gestión del agua de lastre se realizará de conformidad con lo dispuesto en un plan de gestión del agua de lastre aprobado y teniendo en cuenta las Directrices[*] elaboradas por la Organización.

---

[*] Véanse las Directrices para el control y la gestión del agua de lastre de los buques a fin de reducir al mínimo la transferencia de organismos acuáticos perjudiciales y agentes patógenos, adoptadas por la Organización mediante la resolución A.868(20).

3   Anotaciones en el Libro registro del agua de lastre

Se efectuarán las siguientes anotaciones en el Libro registro del agua de lastre en cada una de las ocasiones que se indican a continuación:

3.1   Cuando se tome agua de lastre a bordo:

.1   Fecha, hora y lugar del puerto o instalación donde se efectúa la toma (puerto o latitud/longitud), profundidad (si es fuera del puerto)

.2   Volumen aproximado de la toma en metros cúbicos

.3   Firma del oficial encargado de la operación.

3.2   Cuando se haga circular o se trate agua de lastre a los efectos de la gestión del agua de lastre:

.1   Fecha y hora de la operación

.2   Volumen aproximado circulado o tratado (en metros cúbicos)

.3   Indicación de si la operación se ha llevado a cabo de acuerdo con el plan de gestión del agua de lastre

.4   Firma del oficial encargado de la operación.

3.3   Cuando se descargue agua de lastre en el mar:

.1   Fecha, hora y lugar del puerto o instalación donde se efectúa la descarga (puerto o latitud/longitud)

.2   Volumen aproximado del agua descargada en metros cúbicos más volumen restante en metros cúbicos

.3   Indicación de si se había aplicado o no, antes de la descarga, el plan de gestión del agua de lastre aprobado

.4   Firma del oficial encargado de la operación.

3.4   Cuando se descargue agua de lastre en una instalación de recepción:

.1   Fecha, hora y lugar de la toma

.2   Fecha, hora y lugar de la descarga

.3   Puerto o instalación

.4   Volumen aproximado del agua descargada o tomada, en metros cúbicos

.5   Indicación de si se había aplicado o no, antes de la descarga, el plan de gestión del agua de lastre aprobado

.6   Firma del oficial encargado de la operación.

3.5   Cuando se produzca una descarga o toma accidental o excepcional de agua de lastre:

.1   Fecha y hora del acaecimiento

.2   Puerto o situación del buque en el momento del acaecimiento

.3   Volumen aproximado del agua de lastre descargada

.4   Circunstancias de la toma, descarga, fuga o pérdida, razones de la misma y observaciones generales

.5   Indicación de si se había aplicado o no, antes de la descarga, el plan de gestión del agua de lastre aprobado

.6   Firma del oficial encargado de la operación.

3.6   Procedimientos operacionales adicionales y observaciones generales

4   Volumen del agua de lastre

El volumen de agua de lastre que haya a bordo debería calcularse en metros cúbicos. El Libro registro del agua de lastre contiene numerosas referencias al volumen aproximado de agua de lastre. Se admite que la precisión en el cálculo de esos volúmenes de agua de lastre es susceptible de interpretación.

REGISTRO DE LAS OPERACIONES RELACIONADAS CON EL AGUA DE LASTRE

PÁGINA DE MUESTRA DEL LIBRO REGISTRO DEL AGUA DE LASTRE

Nombre del buque . . . .

Número o letras distintivos . . . .

Fecha	Dato (número)	Registro de las operaciones/ firma de los oficiales a cargo

Firma del capitán . . . .

DOCUMENTO ADJUNTO

RESOLUCIONES ADOPTADAS POR LA CONFERENCIA

Resolución 1

Labor futura de la Organización respecto del Convenio internacional para el control y la gestión del agua de lastre y los sedimentos de los buques

LA CONFERENCIA,

HABIENDO ADOPTADO el Convenio internacional para el control y la gestión del agua de lastre y los sedimentos de los buques (el Convenio),

TOMANDO NOTA de que los artículos 5 y 9 y las reglas A-4, A-5, B-1, B-3, B-4, B-5, C-1, D-3 y D-4 del anexo del Convenio remiten a las directrices o procedimientos que elaborará la Organización para los fines concretos en ellos indicados,

RECONOCIENDO la necesidad de elaborar esas directrices con el fin de garantizar una aplicación uniforme a escala mundial de las correspondientes prescripciones del Convenio,

INVITA a la Organización a que elabore con carácter de urgencia:

.1 las directrices sobre las instalaciones de recepción de sedimentos previstas en el artículo 5 y en la regla B-5;

.2 las directrices para el muestreo del agua de lastre previstas en el artículo 9;

.3 las directrices sobre el cumplimiento equivalente de la gestión del agua de lastre para las embarcaciones de recreo y de búsqueda y salvamento previstas en la regla A-5;

.4 las directrices sobre el plan de gestión del agua de lastre previstas en la regla B-1;

.5 las directrices sobre las instalaciones de recepción del agua de lastre previstas en la regla B-3;

.6 las directrices para el cambio de agua de lastre previstas en la regla B-4;

.7 las directrices sobre las medidas adicionales previstas en la regla C-1 y sobre la evaluación de riesgos previstas en la regla A-4;

.8 las directrices para la aprobación de los sistemas de gestión del agua de lastre previstas en la regla D-3.1;

.9 el procedimiento para la aprobación de sustancias activas previsto en la regla D 3.2; y

.10 las directrices sobre los prototipos de tecnologías para el tratamiento del agua de lastre previstas en la regla D-4,

y las adopte tan pronto como sea posible, y en cualquier caso antes de la entrada en vigor del Convenio, con miras a facilitar una implantación uniforme a escala mundial del mismo.

Resolución 2

Uso de instrumentos de decisión para examinar las normas de conformidad con la regla D-5

LA CONFERENCIA,

HABIENDO ADOPTADO el Convenio internacional para el control y la gestión del agua de lastre y los sedimentos de los buques (el Convenio),

TOMANDO NOTA de que la regla D-5 del Convenio estipula que en una reunión del Comité de Protección del Medio Marino que se celebrará a más tardar tres años antes de la fecha más temprana de entrada en vigor de la norma descrita en la regla D-2, el Comité llevará a cabo un examen que, entre otras cosas, determine si se dispone de las tecnologías adecuadas para el cumplimiento de dicha norma y evalúe los criterios del párrafo 2 de la regla D-5 y las repercusiones socioeconómicas específicamente en relación con las necesidades de desarrollo de los países en desarrollo, especialmente de los pequeños Estados insulares en desarrollo,

RECONOCIENDO el valor que tienen los instrumentos de decisión cuando se realizan evaluaciones complejas,

RECOMIENDA a la Organización que use instrumentos de decisión apropiados cuando efectúe el examen de las normas prescrito por la regla D-5 del Convenio; y

INVITA a los Estados Miembros a que informen a la Organización de cualquier instrumento de decisión eficaz que pueda facilitarle tal examen.

Resolución 3

Fomento de la cooperación y la asistencia técnica

LA CONFERENCIA,

HABIENDO ADOPTADO el Convenio internacional para el control y la gestión del agua de lastre y los sedimentos de los buques (el Convenio),

CONSCIENTE de que las Partes en el Convenio tendrán que dar plena y completa efectividad a las disposiciones de éste, a fin de prevenir, reducir al mínimo y, en último término, eliminar la transferencia de organismos acuáticos perjudiciales y agentes patógenos mediante el control y la gestión del agua de lastre y los sedimentos de los buques,

TOMANDO NOTA de que el Convenio, en sus artículos 13.1 y 13.2, estipula que las Partes, entre otras cosas, facilitarán apoyo a las Partes que soliciten asistencia técnica respecto del control y la gestión del agua de lastre y los sedimentos de los buques,

RECONOCIENDO el valor de las actividades de cooperación técnica llevadas a cabo desde 2000 en asociación con países en desarrollo sobre cuestiones relativas a la gestión del agua de lastre en el marco del Programa mundial de gestión del agua de lastre FMAM/PNUD/OMI (GloBallast),

CONVENCIDA de que el fomento de la cooperación técnica acelerará la aceptación, interpretación uniforme y ejecución del Convenio por los Estados,

TOMANDO NOTA CON AGRADECIMIENTO de que, mediante la aprobación de la resolución A.901(21), la Asamblea de la Organización Marítima Internacional (OMI):

a) afirmó que la labor de la OMI en la elaboración de normas marítimas a escala mundial y en la facilitación de cooperación técnica a fin de implantar y hacer cumplir de manera eficaz dichas normas puede contribuir, y de hecho contribuye, al desarrollo sostenible; y

b) decidió que la misión de la OMI por lo que respecta a la cooperación técnica a partir del año 2000 es ayudar a los países en desarrollo a reforzar su capacidad para cumplir las reglas y normas internacionales relativas a la seguridad marítima y a la prevención y contención de la contaminación del mar, otorgando prioridad a los programas de asistencia técnica que se centran en el desarrollo de los recursos humanos, particularmente a través de la formación, y la creación de capacidad institucional,

1.   PIDE a los Estados Miembros que, en colaboración con la OMI, otros Estados y órganos internacionales interesados, las organizaciones internacionales o regionales competentes y los programas del sector, fomenten y

faciliten, directamente o a través de la OMI, el apoyo necesario a los Estados que soliciten asistencia técnica para:

a) la evaluación de las repercusiones de la ratificación, aceptación o aprobación del Convenio, o de la adhesión al mismo, así como de la implantación y ejecución de éste;

b) la elaboración de la legislación nacional y las disposiciones institucionales necesarias para dar efecto al Convenio;

c) la formación de personal científico y técnico para tareas de investigación, vigilancia y ejecución (por ejemplo, evaluaciones de los riesgos del agua de lastre, estudios de especies marinas invasoras, sistemas de vigilancia y alerta temprana, y muestreo y análisis del agua de lastre), que incluya, según proceda, el suministro de las instalaciones y el equipo necesarios, con miras a fortalecer las capacidades nacionales;

d) el intercambio de información y cooperación técnica respecto de la reducción al mínimo de los riesgos para el medio ambiente y la salud de los seres humanos debidos a la transferencia de organismos acuáticos perjudiciales y agentes patógenos mediante el control y la gestión del agua de lastre y los sedimentos de los buques;

e) la investigación y el desarrollo de mejores métodos de gestión y tratamiento del agua de lastre; y

f) el establecimiento de prescripciones especiales en determinadas zonas de conformidad con la sección C de las reglas del Convenio;

2.   PIDE ADEMÁS a los organismos y organizaciones internacionales de desarrollo que brinden apoyo, incluida la provisión de los recursos necesarios, a los programas de cooperación técnica en el ámbito del control y la gestión del agua de lastre, en consonancia con lo dispuesto en el Convenio;

3.   INVITA al Comité de Cooperación Técnica de la OMI a que siga previendo actividades de creación de capacidad para el control y la gestión del agua de lastre y los sedimentos de los buques en el Programa integrado de cooperación técnica de la Organización, con el fin de apoyar la implantación y el cumplimiento efectivos del Convenio por los países en desarrollo; y

4.   INSTA a todos los Estados a que inicien las actividades relacionadas con las medidas de cooperación técnica antes mencionadas sin esperar a que el Convenio entre en vigor.

Resolución 4

Examen del anexo del Convenio internacional para el control y la gestión del agua de lastre y los sedimentos de los buques

LA CONFERENCIA,

HABIENDO ADOPTADO el Convenio internacional para el control y la gestión del agua de lastre y los sedimentos de los buques (el Convenio),

RECONOCIENDO que el examen del anexo del Convenio, y en particular, aunque esta relación no sea exhaustiva, el de las reglas A-4, A-5, B-1, B-3, B-4, C-1, D-1, D-2, D-3 y D-5, tal vez tenga que estudiarse antes de la entrada en vigor del Convenio, por ejemplo porque se perciban impedimentos para la entrada en vigor o para tratar las normas descritas en la regla D-2 del anexo del Convenio,

RECOMIENDA que el Comité de Protección del Medio Marino examine las reglas del anexo del Convenio según estime oportuno, pero a más tardar tres años antes de la fecha más temprana de entrada en vigor de las normas descritas en la regla D-2 del anexo del Convenio, es decir el año 2006.